WITHDRAWN

FASHION AND SURREALISM

FASHION AND SURREALISM

FASHION AND

SURREALISM

RICHARD MARTIN

RIZZOLI
NEW YORK

First published in the United States of America in 1987 by
Rizzoli International Publications, Inc.
597 Fifth Avenue, New York, NY 10017

Library of Congress Cataloging-in-Publication Data
Martin, Richard
    Fashion and Surrealism
    "Published in conjunction with an exhibition at the Fashion
Institute of Technology, October 30, 1987–January 23, 1988."
    Includes Index.
    1. Fashion. 2. Surrealism. 3. Wearable Art.
I. Fashion Institute of Technology (New York, N.Y.)
II. Title
TT507.M375 1987   709'.04'063   87–4533
ISBN 0–8478–0831–9

PAGES 2–3
MAN RAY (American, 1890–1976)
*Beautiful as the Fortuitous Encounter on a
Dissecting Table of a Sewing Machine and an
Umbrella*, 1933
Photograph
Man Ray Archives, Paris

PAGES 4–5
THIERRY MUGLER
Bird Dresses with Bird Cage, 1982
Photograph Scott Heiser

Edited by Jane Fluegel
Design by Charles Davey
Composition by Rainsford Type, Ridgefield, Connecticut
Printed and bound by Toppan Printing Co., Inc., Japan

CONTENTS

INTRODUCTION

The Surrealist revolution was, like any other, dressed in style. The first generation of Surrealists—André Breton, Paul Eluard, Louis Aragon, and others, who founded the movement in the 1920s—in the ardor and rigor of their definitions and exclusions may not have concerned themselves with the garb of their revolutionary pose, but Surrealism's impulse and compulsion to revolt was necessarily accompanied by fashion suitable to the revolution. Moreover, the metaphor and meaning of fashion were at the heart of Surrealist visual language and offered a natural correspondence to the physical properties of disfigurement that became apparent in Surrealist style.

As the initial incendiary eruptions of Surrealism reified into an artistic style in the 1930s and thereafter, the fashion arts came to serve as a statement of the Surrealist vision and of the Surrealist faith in the connections between the everyday and the exceptional. Fashion became Surrealism's most compelling friction between the ordinary and extraordinary, between disfigurement and embellishment, body and concept, artifice and the real. Fashion's persistent preoccupation with Surrealism and Surrealism's fascination with fashion serve to identify the insurrection art offers to daily life and the accommodations style can make to the commanding vision of art. That is, art of an inherently revolutionary character can make manifest its ideas in fashion. To some, it may seem difficult to imagine that an art initially composed of concepts and words and subsequently of images generated in the complexities of the intellect and subconscious imagination would have its substantive consequence in the fashion arts, but that political picaresque is neither a denial of Surrealism's values nor a depreciation of the fashion arts. Issues abide as readily and lastingly in dress and its conventions as in any other art. In fact, matters of fashion are especially powerful in their social and political implications and intimate contact with human values.

Concepts may be naked at birth, but they are soon swaddled in realities. The clothing that embraced the naked concepts of Surrealism became the inevitable signifier of the concepts it dressed and addressed. Surrealism's traffic between the interior and exterior worlds was not diminished by the role of apparel in art; rather, the substantive participation of fashion in the definition of Surrealism and Surrealist style—the insinuation of fashion's tissue between the naked and the profane, the nude and the profound—yielded a delicate membrane of vibration between Surrealism's abiding antipodes of art and life.

9

METAPHOR AND METAMORPHOSIS

MAN RAY
Gift, 1921 (replica c. 1958)
Flatiron with metal tacks, 6⅛ × 3⅝ × 4½ in.
The Museum of Modern Art, New York
James Thrall Soby Fund

In the nineteenth century, the depiction of
ironing in art identified the remorseless labor of
women; Man Ray's *Gift* is the ironic Surrealist
object that thwarts its utility and titillates the
imagination.

In the beginning was the word. Surrealism began with the spoken and written word. Its early documents and richly evocative texts testify to an art of theoretical initiatives and verbal foundation. The first-generation Surrealists were, after all, convened by the words of Dada, the ideas of Freud, and the polemics of social conviction about art. While the word plays a resonant role throughout Surrealism, even in the fashion arts, that preoccupation was soon complemented by a fascination with objects. And almost immediately objects were accompanied by the fine arts. Only later, primarily through the premier Surrealists working in Paris in the 1930s, did Surrealism fully seize the fashion arts. But when Surrealism came to fashion it was with fervor. Overtaking the fashion arts with zeal, Surrealism has never left. Ideas about fashion presentation in magazines, window display, and apparel have changed in the intervening years, but Surrealism remains fashion's favorite art.

Fashion and its instruments were at the heart of the Surrealist metaphor, touching on the imagery of woman and the correlation between the world of real objects and the life of objects in the mind. The Surrealist propensity to probe the epic description by Isidore Ducasse, Comte de Lautréamont, of the beautiful as "the chance encounter of a sewing machine and an umbrella on a dissecting table" reveals Surrealism's need for language, imagery, and fashion. The recourse to Lautréamont, in a line from his poem *Les Chants de Maldoror* (1868–70), is also indicative of the Surrealist fascination with the heritage of French literary Symbolism of the nineteenth century. As the Surrealists would have it, beauty comes by chance because of the innately superior conditions of the subconscious to those that are controlled and regulated by reason. The rational would always subjugate the true impulses of language, the Surrealists assert, but for the unanticipated, the extraordinary, and the aleatory. Lautréamont's example depends upon the trio of objects as well as their juxtaposition. His description was used both literally and evocatively by the American artist Man Ray. In his photograph *Beautiful as the Fortuitous Encounter on a Dissecting Table of a Sewing Machine and an Umbrella* (1933; frontispiece), he saw the image in a clear-eyed manner, almost banal in its obvious depiction of an odd juxtaposition. In the sculpture *The Enigma of Isidore Ducasse* (1920; pp. 12–13), Man Ray offered his vision clairvoyantly and mystically, allowing us to understand the contents of the work by what we know intellectually and by our assumptions based on the title. Even as we believe we know what lies beneath the hemp and twine, 11 the shape maintains its hulking uncertainty. Like Surrealism in general, the object cherishes its secrecy. The dissecting table, in its uninflected whiteness, variously interpreted as the bed and the clear plane of examination, provides the place of confrontation for the umbrella, symbol of the male, and the sewing machine, an updating of the distaff as symbol of the female. Furthermore, the sewing machine could represent the female worker who in the early years of this century worked in the clothing industry, but it could also represent woman's industriousness in the home in the task of providing dress. Becoming an easy aphorism for Surrealist chance and juxtaposition, the encounter proposed by Lautréamont establishes the sewing machine as an essential surrogate for the woman. Its process is deemed female and its consequence—fashion—is also preeminently female. When Man Ray attempted to give a mysterious presence to the poetic encounter in *The Enigma of Isidore Ducasse*, he created a visual sign, even in its absence of sight within, for the poet's declaration. What poetry had thereby declared to be possible, art could substantiate.

But the sewing machine and its products were not invisible in the Surrealist world. The technology of the machine held its own special allure for the artists of the modern revolution, and the sewing machine itself was a palpable presence. Joseph Cornell, the American artist who became famous for his idiosyncratic Surrealist-inspired collages, was employed in the 1930s as a textile designer for the Traphagen Commercial Textile Studio in New York. There he recognized the sewing machine as an instrument of fabrication and fantasy. The sewing machine makes the clothing, but it also makes the woman, as if sewn/sown from the fruition of the machine. Cornell's understanding of the fertility of the sewing machine was already apparent in his untitled 1931 collage (p. 15), subsequently published in *Harper's Bazaar* as one of two images dealing with sewing; in them the sewing machine creates not only the garment but also the woman within it. In the background, women work at sewing machines along an assembly line. Flowers and corn appear as the raw materials of textile and ultimately of the fashionable woman who emerges as the machine's creation. Redolent of the Lautréamont metaphor for beauty, Cornell's model *ex machina* is fashion's creation from the raw and psychologically charged materials of the sewing machine. Cornell shared with many Surrealists an obsession with the image of woman and a reticence about women. Such contradictory impulses in image-making could be reconciled by the sewing machine as woman's symbol.

The sewing machine had always been present in the Surrealist vision, from an early occurrence in an object, *Here Lies Giorgio de Chirico* (reproduced in *La Révolution Surréaliste*, March 15, 1928), by Louis Aragon and André Breton, which places a small sewing machine in front of a model of the Tower of Pisa, through such examples as Salvador Dali's catalog cover for an exhibition of his prints at the Julien Levy Gallery in New York in 1934 (an early and critical Surrealist exhibition in the United States) and a sewing machine within a landscape in the Prague Surrealist bulletin of April 9, 1935. What Man Ray saw within the enigma of a package, Oscar Dominguez viewed as specifically sexual in his *Electrosexual Sewing Machine* (1934; p. 14), again with the woman and fertility as the machine's production. In a 1934 edition of Lautréamont's *Chants de Maldoror* (p. 15), Dali illustrates the sewing machine in the process of creating woman, a me-

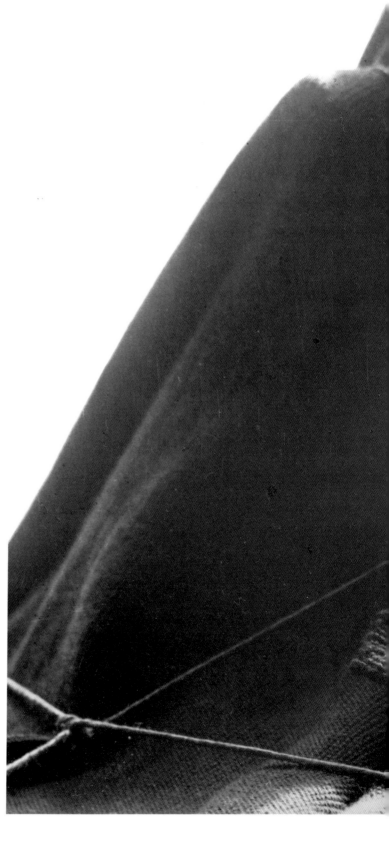

MAN RAY (American, 1890–1976)
The Enigma of Isidore Ducasse, 1920 (replica 1967)
Cloth and rope over sewing machine, 16 in. high
The Museum of Modern Art, New York
Study Collection

Provocative, mysterious, the Man Ray photograph (PAGES 2–3) and object are based on a line from *Les Chants de Maldoror* by the nineteenth-century French poet Isidore Ducasse, who wrote under the name "Comte de Lautréamont." Published by André Breton in *Littérature* in 1919, Ducasse's text offered a premise for the Surrealist examination of objects, particularly the sewing machine.

OSCAR DOMINGUEZ (French, born
Spain, 1906–1957)
Electrosexual Sewing Machine, 1934
Oil on canvas, 39 ⅛ × 31 ⅝ in.
Private collection, Paris

Enigmatic, erotic, even exploitative,
Dominguez's perception of the sewing machine
draws on other Surrealist objects.

chanistic version of the tale from Genesis. The God-Creator for Dali is the male force, not necessarily the Godhead, but the male who creates, cannibalizes, and controls. To the aphorism that clothes make the man, the Surrealists offered their alternative: the sewing machine makes the woman. By extension, the beauty residing in the woman—and all those other forces the Surrealists associated with beauty and with women—was the compression of clothing and form as if indissolubly sewn together. Sown and sewn by man and machine, woman emerges clothed.

Max Ernst anticipated the Surrealist fascination with fashion in his 1919 lithographs *Fiat modes, pereat ars* (Let There Be Fashion, Down with Art; p. 16), a suite of fashion plates that are a justification of the mode as well as its humor. Undeniably important within the Ernst oeuvre, these lithographs show the artist's stylistic affinity to Giorgio de Chirico and derivation of the mannequin surrogate for the human figure from the Italian artist. De Chirico stood as a precursor to the Surrealists rather than a colleague, but his role was essential to the Surrealist imaging of woman in an inanimate form. That de Chirico's particular interest was the mannequin is a commitment to the possibility of fashion as human metaphor. The de Chirico mannequin is both an individual and a standard, both a single human being and the generic human.

Ernst played with the significance of luxury and fashion, substituting *fiat modes* for the more likely *fiat lux* (let there be light, of biblical text, but recognizing the equivalence of *luxe* and *mode* as interpretations of fashion. His express denial of art and ostensible preference for fashion avow a sense of the freshness and changing aspect of fashion, not an undesirable quality to Ernst and many others involved with Dada and Surrealism. Because fashion presented a more ephemeral artistic mode, it enjoyed an advantage over the obdurate and

unchanging aspects of the fine arts. The mechanistic fantasies of mannequins, machines, quasi-equations, and animated dress forms provided Ernst with the translation of the mechanical devices favored by Dada into a more implicitly humanized or anthropomorphic art preferred by the Surrealists. It is as if Goya's image of the mannequin as surrogate for the human being was being brought into the new century and a new context. The precise measurements and anthropometric calculations of *Fiat modes* offer another device in fashion's comprehension and metamorphosis. Whereas Vitruvian theory and the Renaissance study of perspective had placed man and his optic at the center of all quantification and viewing, Ernst placed the mannequin there as the measure of all that surrounds. To see the tailor as the artist and the mannequin as form is to make of Pygmalion a story about clothing. In declaring *pereat ars*, Ernst denounced the pretension of the fine arts in favor of the creative energy of fashion. Although this gesture was finally no more than a symbolic action on Ernst's part, it permitted subsequent artists to present their work in "low art" formats, like that of the lithograph on inexpensive paper utilized in *Fiat modes*. Ernst proffered the possibility of mistaking his art for a sales catalog, a commerical advertisement, or the popular newspaper and magazine representations of fashion that were becoming commonplace in the new century. It is, then, not entirely startling to realize that in 1927 and 1928 Belgian Surrealist artist René Magritte illustrated the fur catalogs for Maison Samuel, a fashionable boutique in Brussels (p. 17). Commercial fashion art and illustration could hardly be an inappropriate enterprise if Ernst had sought fashion's effects while ennobling its functions. Twentieth-century ready-to-wear has generated substantial popular imagery through advertising, and that imagery was examined and plundered not only by Surrealism but also by Cubist collage. Moreover, Ernst's particular depictions of fashion addressed its internationalism, employing texts in French, German, and Latin along with mathematical formulas. If fashion were wholly frivolous, as some would have it, then its representation could hardly be so linked with languages of cognition and expression.

Ernst's appropriation of images from commerce is also evident in his collage *The Hat Makes the Man* (1920; p. 18). A work of pasted paper with its constituent elements taken from popular advertising for men's hats, it offers the repetitions found in commerce as a means to art. Further, the variations on the hat suggest its inference as psychic synecdoche, Freud having readily identified the man with his hat. Although the Surrealists refused to grant Freud the literal accuracy of his interpretation of symbols, they used many of his psychoanalytic constructions to advance their own intuitions of meaning. Thus, in a popular image—and a popular expression—Ernst realized the dramatic and suggestive potential of the fashion object, but also that moment when the article of clothing is the metaphor, metamorphosis, and metaphysics of the man.

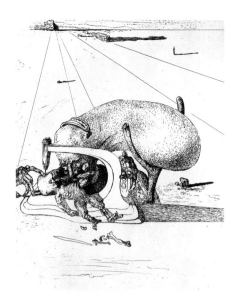

LEFT
SALVADOR DALI (Spanish, born 1904)
Plate 14 from *Les Chants de Maldoror*, by the
Comte de Lautréamont, 1934
Etching, 13 ⅛ × 10 ⅛ in. (sheet)
The Museum of Modern Art, New York
The Louis E. Stern Collection

The sewing machine was a sinister, saturnine,
diabolical, and even destroying machine in
Dali's imagination.

BELOW
JOSEPH CORNELL (American, 1903–
1972)
Untitled, 1931
Collage, 5 ¼ × 8 ⅛ in.
Published *Harper's Bazaar*, New York,
February 1937

Reproduced under the rubric "The Pulse of
Fashion," Cornell's collage was the embodiment
of woman as garment and of the sewing
machine as creative enterprise.

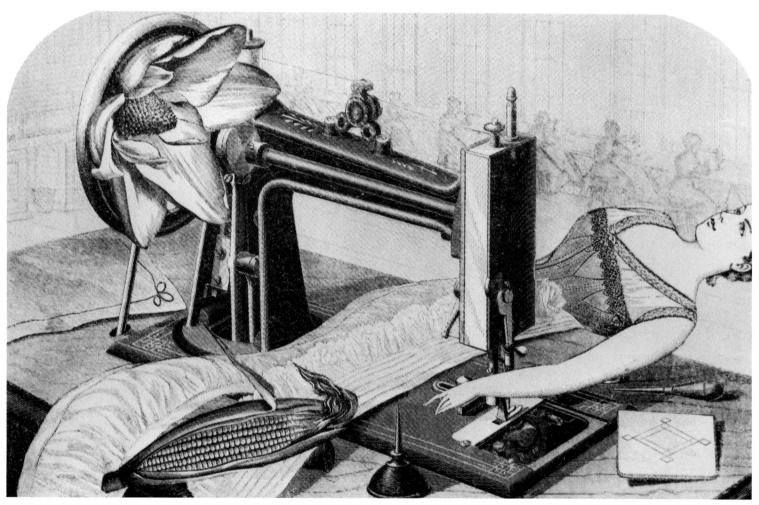

Likewise, two images of hats photographed by Man Ray in the 1930s (p. 18) and published together in an article by Tristan Tzara in *Minotaure* (more or less a house journal of Surrealism), in 1933, may indicate the specific interpretive possibilities of fashion even, as contemporary critic Rosalind Krauss has pointed out, in the paradoxical relationship between the camera's witness and the Surrealist vision. In an article devoted to the automatism of taste, Tzara contended that a certain large hat with an opening was specifically vaginal and that hats could be argued to be expressions of specific conscious and unconscious ideas. In these instances, the hat makes the woman in every regard. The brim of a hat may obscure the wearer, resulting in the disfigurement or literal disembodiment of the hat, thus casting it on its own as an item of apparel and as a symbol. The crease or crevice of the hat becomes both an abstract field and a symbol offered in association with eye and gender. Correspondingly, the hat

with a tip can be construed as Surrealist symbol and genitalia when it is sufficiently dissociated from the figure to become its own independent object.

The isolating, modifying, and comprehending of ordinary objects and their meanings had been sanctioned by the Surrealist movement's Dada progenitors. In the transition from Dada to Surrealism, the object provided an important harmony, suggesting that all things, even those achieved by chance or presented in new associations or radical dissociations, could be said to have meaning. Furthermore, the artistic sanctification of the ordinary object could challenge customary definitions of art as a lofty and separate achievement. Accorded radical autonomy in Surrealist theory and art, the object could be the surrogate of the figure, and it could be the powerful expression of all that is unseen and/or unexpressed in a given image. The fashion object, like the fashion machine, could be a most powerful force in the simul- 15

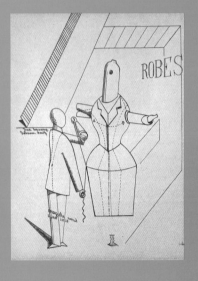

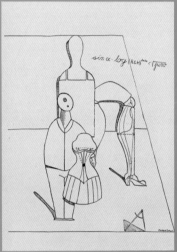

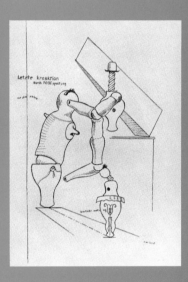

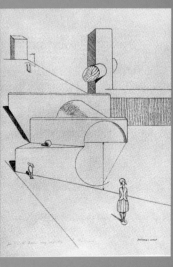

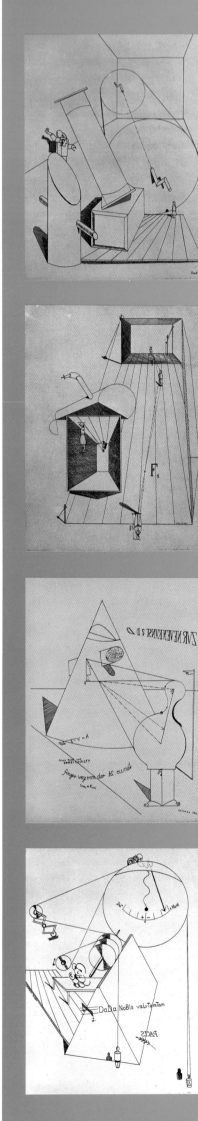

MAX ERNST (French, born Germany, 1891–1976)
Plates from *Fiat modes, pereat ars* (Let There Be Fashion, Down with Art), 1919
Lithographs, each 17 15/16 × 13 in. (sheet)
The Museum of Modern Art, New York
Purchase Fund

Working in Cologne in 1919, Dada artist Max Ernst pronounced the dressmaker's art to be the equal of, if not superior to, the fine arts. *Fiat modes*, a portfolio of eight lithographs, adopts the mannequin figures of Giorgio de Chirico's Metaphysical paintings but transforms them into creations that are uniquely Ernst's own.

taneous deconstruction of the figure and remembrance of its presence that inevitably dwells in the garment. The fashion-related objects of Surrealism include Man Ray's somewhat sinister *Gift* (1921; replica p. 10), as well as hangers, thimbles, scissors, and mannequins and dress forms.

"Music remains confined," de Chirico had written in disparagement of the power of music to carry the full meaning of the Surrealist impulse. Nonetheless, music played a role in the Surrealist imagination, most especially in the form of musical instruments, which were thought to bear resemblances to women. The objectification of woman (the notion of woman as object), would include the concept of woman as surrogate musical instrument, posed by Man Ray in *Le Violon d'Ingres* (1924; p. 19). The woman as stringed instrument became a preoccupation of many Surrealist artists, including Salvador Dali, as in his *Flamenco Dancer* (1949–50; p. 22). From these postulations, the transference to fashion was a simple matter. If the shape of the body could be seen as similar to the stringed instrument, then the body could take on the form of the instrument as in Karl Lagerfeld's design for Chloe (1983; p. 35) and Christian Lacroix's creation for Jean Patou (1985; p. 24) of dresses that fulfill the concept of Man Ray. The presence of music in another form is also important to the possibility of realizing the absolute and the mysterious through the visible and real. The Romantic synaesthesia that sought transference among the senses could also allow music to serve as a metaphor for woman; siren and muse in the photographs of Serge Lutens (pp. 21, 33, 34), she might stand for perfection in sound as well as for visual beauty. Musical notes describe form in Valentine Hugo's program design (1941; p. 22), but so too does music become form in the musical-notation dress (1937; p. 25) designed by Elsa Schiaparelli and the ode to the treble clef (1984; p. 22) designed by Dominique Lacoustille. As a form that has presence yet is invisible, music held some intrigue for the Surrealists and necessarily had its role in their depiction of woman as musical form. In dress, it had its harmony as well.

Just as music could be envisioned as both an abstract form and a physical presence, so too the biomorphic abstractions that characterize much Surrealist art found their way into the free forms of dress and the definition of the human being as an abstract flow among units of the body. What could seem almost nonrepresentational in some Surrealist art became in

RENE MAGRITTE (Belgian, 1898–1967)
Pages from Fur Catalog for La Maison Samuel,
Brussels, 1928

Surrealist painter Magritte, commissioned by a
Brussels store in both 1927 and 1928 to create
its winter fur catalog, closely followed the style
of his mysterious paintings in his fashion
advertising.

Dali's hands mutations on the body bulbous, emaciated, or
elongated, with the parts of the body achieving a new order
and dynamic in accordance with their psychosexual role as
perceived by Dali. The Surrealism of sculptor Jean Arp, as in
his *Nose-Cheeks* (1925–26; p. 30) and *Human Concretion*
(1933; p. 28), and later of painter Yves Tanguy, as in *Multiplication of the Arcs* (1954; pp. 26–27), which lacked the
narrative and representational modes found in the work of
their colleagues Dali and Magritte, did not immediately influence dress. In the 1980s, however, it came to affect many
designers who sought an abstraction that might surpass the
conventional description of the body in an analytical anatomy. Georgina Godley's highly conceptual Shaped Underwear and Shaped Dress (both 1986; pp. 29, 31) reorder and
abstract forms derived from the body. Put to the extreme test
of adapting purely abstract, biomorphic form to a manner of
dress compatible with human anatomy, fashion has risen to
the challenge with humor in the 1985 dresses of Olivier Guillemin (pp. 26, 27) and with élan in the carefully wrought
sleeve of a 1984 Claude Montana coat (p. 30). Fashion is, like
art, capable of abstractions.

Seeking marvels and realizing dreams, the artists and designers of Surrealism came to illusionism and to deceits of the eye
as primary devices for both concealing and revealing the marvelous in a mundane world. To René Magritte, his *Magic
Mirror* (1928–29; p. 46) seemed to be a place wherein the
reality reflected became an act of imagination. In *Not to Be
Reproduced* (1937; p. 44), the framed mirror enjoys an
ironic relationship with the framed picture in its representation of the purportedly real. In *The Human Condition, I*
(1934; p. 44), picture window and picture frame coincide,
providing variable elements in the determination of a Surrealist reality. Magritte's passive observers in an absurd world
and his lambent observations on perceived worlds within
frames made vexing mirror pictures.

The superior image of the mirror obtained in clothing as in
art, with mirrors appearing as creative fastenings on an Elsa
Schiaparelli jacket (p. 38) and as a pictorial device on one by
Yves Saint Laurent (p. 39). But the mirror is only part of the
fantasy of reflections on appearance and illusion engaged in
by these designers. The creation of illusion, whether of a figure, candelabrum, or mirror, gives to clothing the full fran-
chise of art, allowing implications of narrative, mystery, and
deep reflection to occur as a function of dress. The vesting of

clothing with this figurative and fantasied role marks Surrealism's assimilation into dress. In photography, the process is manifest in works by Cecil Beaton and Horst P. Horst (pp. 42, 43), who manipulate the spectator by creating an ambiguity between what is literally within the picture and the reality outside the image. In painting, the same possibilities for adjusted spectatorship prevail—whether to establish the certainties of perceived realities and the security of a fixed position for the observer or, in Surrealism, to exacerbate the uncertainties of both. But dress that plays with the real and unreal is all but unanticipated. The mirror of vanity and dress was shattered by the reflections and revelations of Surrealism.

OPPOSITE
MAN RAY
Le Violon d'Ingres, 1924 (1971)
Photograph with collage
Man Ray Archives, Paris
Published *Littérature*, Paris, June 1924

Man Ray's vision of woman as musical instrument satirizes the Cubist obsession with the guitar and the Ingresque obsession with the odalisque. The process of synaesthesia between music and physical beauty is perfectly realized in this portrait of Kiki de Montparnasse.

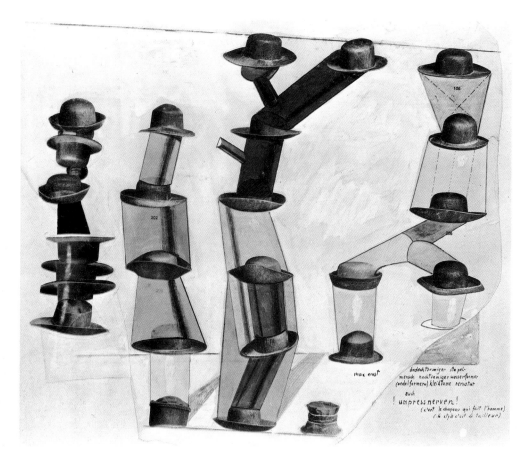

LEFT
MAX ERNST
The Hat Makes the Man, 1920
Collage, pencil, ink, and watercolor on paper, 14 × 18 in.
The Museum of Modern Art, New York
Purchase Fund

Using elements from a commercial advertisement for hats, Ernst's collage, realizing the cliché, once more nods to the significance of fashion.

BOTTOM LEFT AND RIGHT
MAN RAY
Illustrations for "A Certain Automatism of Taste," by Tristan Tzara, published *Minotaure*, Paris, 1933
Photographs
Collection Rosabianca Skira, Geneva

Ernst believed that the hat made the man, but Man Ray and Tristan Tzara, switching gender, saw woman embodied in the hat, a Tiresian reversal.

LEFT
PAUL COLIN (French, born Russia, 1905–1986)
L'Orchestre en Liberté: Costume for the Violin (worn by Serge Lifar), 1933
Charcoal and gouache on paper, 23 5/16 × 15 1/8 in.
Wadsworth Atheneum, Hartford, Connecticut
From the Serge Lifar Collection, the Ella Gallup Sumner and Mary Catlin Sumner Collection

BELOW
PAUL COLIN
L'Orchestre en Liberté: Costume for Two Woodwinds, 1931
Charcoal and gouache on two sheets of paper, 23 1/2 × 15 1/4 in.
Wadsworth Atheneum, Hartford, Connecticut
From the Serge Lifar Collection, the Ella Gallup Sumner and Mary Catlin Sumner Collection

On February 16, 1931, Serge Lifar's ballet *L'Orchestre en Liberté*, its costumes designed by Paul Colin, opened at the Paris Opera. Colin animated the entire orchestra as living instruments, giving form to the music of composer Henri Sauveplane.

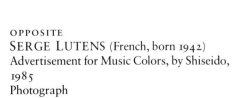

OPPOSITE
SERGE LUTENS (French, born 1942)
Advertisement for Music Colors, by Shiseido, 1985
Photograph

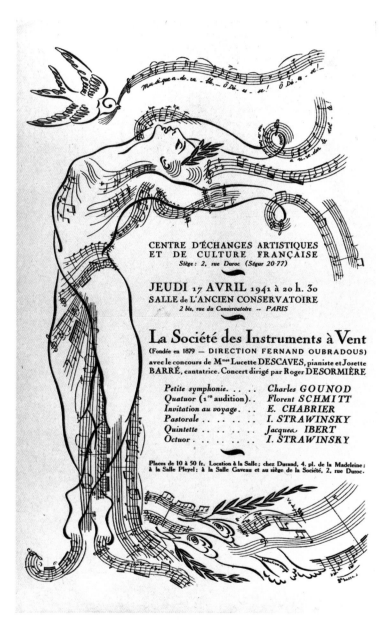

CENTRE D'ÉCHANGES ARTISTIQUES
ET DE CULTURE FRANÇAISE
Siège : 2, rue Duroc (Ségur 20-77)

JEUDI 17 AVRIL 1941 à 20 h. 30
SALLE de L'ANCIEN CONSERVATOIRE
2 bis, rue du Conservatoire -- PARIS

La Société des Instruments à Vent
(Fondée en 1879 — DIRECTION FERNAND OUBRADOUS)
avec le concours de Mmes Lucette DESCAVES, pianiste et Josette
BARRÉ, cantatrice. Concert dirigé par Roger DESORMIÈRE

Petite symphonie. . . .	Charles GOUNOD
Quatuor (1re audition). .	Florent SCHMITT
Invitation au voyage. . .	E. CHABRIER
Pastorale	I. STRAWINSKY
Quintette	Jacques IBERT
Octuor	I. STRAWINSKY

Places de 10 à 50 fr. Location à la Salle ; chez Durand, 4. pl. de la Madeleine :
à la Salle Pleyel : à la Salle Gaveau et au siège de la Société, 2, rue Duroc.

L' de Clef de Sol

VALENTINE HUGO (French, 1887–1968)
Program for the Society of Wind Instruments,
Paris, April 17 1941
Collection Anne de Margerie, Paris

Music clothes the figure in artist Hugo's
program design. She took part in Surrealist
exhibitions in Paris in the 1930s.

SALVADOR DALI
Flamenco Dancer, 1949–50
Published *Flair*, New York, March 1950

If Surrealist transformation allowed the body to
be viewed as stringed instrument, it also
permitted the instrument to become the body
making music and dance, the ultimate
synaesthesia.

DOMINIQUE LACOUSTILLE (French,
born 1956)
Treble-Clef Dress, 1984

The young French designer adapts the musical
motif for clothing.

KARL LAGERFELD (French, born
Germany 1938)
Keyboard Belt (for Chloe), 1982
Photograph Roxanne Lowit
Watercolor Antonio Lopez

CHRISTIAN LACROIX (French, born
1951)
Violin Dress (for Jean Patou), 1985
Photograph Horst P. Horst

Photographed in the setting of art, Christian
Lacroix's Violin Dress is a musical evocation in
the spirit of Surrealism.

ELSA SCHIAPARELLI (French, born Italy,
1890–1973)
Musical Notation Dress, 1937
Musée des Arts de la Mode, Paris
Schiaparelli Studio Sketchbooks, U.F.A.C.

Schiaparelli, the designer most influenced by
Surrealism, featured musical scores and
embroidered instruments in her designs for the
spring collection of 1937. Her friendship with
Dada and Surrealist artists Francis Picabia,
Man Ray, Marcel Duchamp, and Tristan Tzara
dated from the early 1920s in Paris.

OLIVIER GUILLEMIN (French, born 1962)
Dress Design, Studio Berçot, Paris, 1985
Photograph Roxanne Lowit

Although the abstract biomorphic forms devised by Surrealist artists Jean Arp and Yves Tanguy are difficult to translate into wearable garments, inventions such as Olivier Guillemin's, while still a student at Studio Berçot, Paris, suggest some possibilities for success.

ABOVE
YVES TANGUY (American, born France,
1900–1955)
Multiplication of the Arcs (detail), 1954
Oil on canvas, 40 × 60 in.
The Museum of Modern Art, New York
Mrs. Simon Guggenheim Fund

OLIVIER GUILLEMIN
Dress Design, Studio Berçot, Paris, 1985
Photograph Roxanne Lowit

JEAN ARP
Human Concretion, 1933
Bronze, 22⅜ × 22⅛ × 13⅞ in.
Private collection. Courtesy Minneapolis
Institute of Arts

Deriving abstraction from recognized human
forms, Arp made possible the emergence of a
new Surrealist anatomy along with a Surrealist
style.

GEORGINA GODLEY (British, born 1955)
Shaped Underwear, 1986
Photograph Cindy Palmano

The distortions of the body imposed in
Surrealist photography and sculpture were, in
part, motivated by eroticism. Godley's designs
perform a like function.

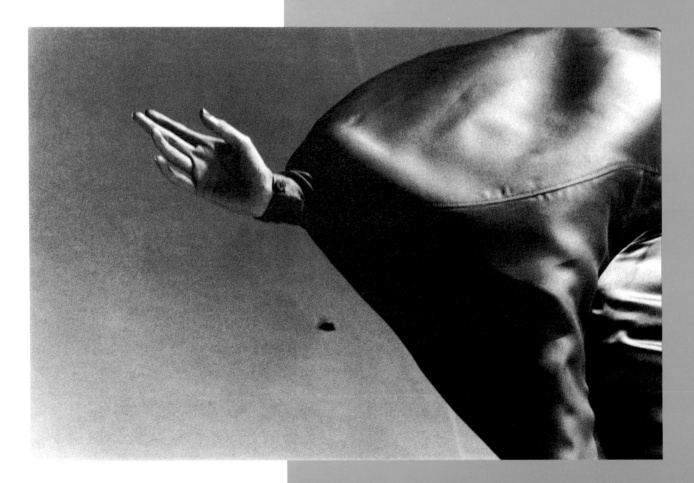

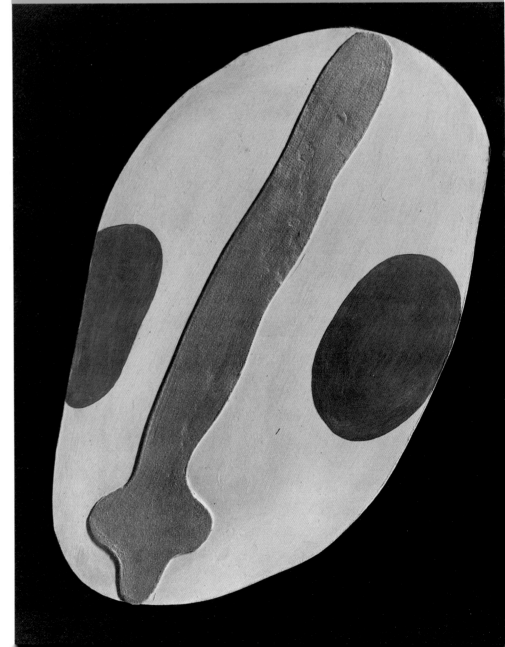

CLAUDE MONTANA (French, born 1949)
Red-Satin Cocoon Coat (detail), 1984
Photograph Scott Heiser

In one of his 1984 collections, Montana
investigated the ballooning, volumetric,
sculptural possibilities of clothing, including
bulbous, Arp-like sleeves and champagne
glasses as figures.

JEAN ARP (French, born Strasbourg, 1887–
1966)
Nose-Cheeks, 1925–26
Painted cardboard relief, 16 ⅛ × 12 ⅜ in.
Galerie Beyeler, Basel

GEORGINA GODLEY
Shaped Dress, 1986
Photograph Cindy Palmano

Cognizant of the history of Surrealist art,
British designer Georgina Godley explores the
possibilities of Surrealist dilation and variation
of the body in fantasies of exaggerated form.

ABOVE
DAVIDE MOSCONI (Italian, born 1941)
Fashion Photograph
Published *Linea Italiana*, Milan, December
1978

The imperatives of the fashion photograph
can prompt distortion of the body to empha-
size the detail over the whole, even with
unsettling Surrealist effects of distension and
repetition.

LEFT
SHEILA ROCK (British)
Leather Coif by Kirsten Woodward, 1986
Photograph

In a millinery tour de force, Woodward
creates the semblance of hair in leather, skin
supplanting coiffure. The photograph by Rock
stresses the biomorphic transformation of the
figure in motion.

OPPOSITE
SERGE LUTENS
Advertisement for Les Rhythmiques, by
Christian Dior, 1979
Photograph

Sheet music, the graphic representation of the
ineffable sounds of music, becomes the physical
presence of clothing.

OPPOSITE
ANTONIO
Guitar Dress, by Karl Lagerfeld (for Chloe), 1983
Watercolor

The dream of *Le Violon d'Ingres* assumes sartorial form in Karl Lagerfeld's design, rendered by fashion illustrator Antonio.

TOP LEFT
LINDA FARGO (American, born 1957)
Window Display, R. H. Macy, New York, 1985

Taking a cue from Surrealism, this window display features mannequins with guitar torsoes.

CENTER LEFT
SERGE LUTENS
Advertisement for Les Rhythmiques, by Christian Dior, 1979
Photograph

BOTTOM LEFT
CANDY PRATTS PRICE (American, born 1950)
Window Display, Bloomingdale's, New York, 1978

American designer and editor Price includes music as a theme in windows for the New York department store.

LEFT
MARIA VITTORIA CORRADI (Italian)
Fashion Photograph
Published *Linea Italiana*, Milan, August 1981

Trompe l'oeil becomes a standard mode in fashion imagery to reveal the fashion and cosmetic process. The cosmetics jars are an artifice, but they are "real," in the sense of being three-dimensional objects placed on photographic illusions.

OPPOSITE
SERGE LUTENS
Baroque and Poesy Advertising Campaign for Inoui, by Shiseido, 1985
Photograph

Beauty is framed within the illusionism of living forms, a suspension of disbelief, and a splendid suspension of the image. Promotion of a line of Japanese cosmetics is the purpose of the campaign.

BELOW
Fashion Photograph
Published *Linea Italiana*, Milan, April 1981
KOSAK

Reality emerges from the mirrors and strides into illusion, two sides of the same mirror.

ELSA SCHIAPARELLI
Rococo Mirror Jacket, 1939
The Metropolitan Museum of Art, New York
The Costume Institute, Gift of Baroness
Philippe de Rothschild
Photograph Taishi Hirokawa

Rococo hand mirrors with fractured faces
frame the breasts and suggest a window view
into the figure. The shattering of the mirrors
may be the only means to preclude visual entry
into the garment. Schiaparelli offers the
garment at its most provocative, rupturing
decorum, almost seeing within and seeing
reflections, and ending ironically with a
cracked set of mirrors.

OPPOSITE
YVES SAINT LAURENT (French, born
Algeria 1936)
Rococo Mirror Jacket, 1978–79
Photograph Claus Ohm

Although the mirror has migrated on the body,
its mystery of imaging and its broken invisibility
remain. The cracked glass is reflective of the
phantasmagorical Surrealism of Jean Cocteau
and Cecil Beaton. The embroidery is executed
by the House of Lesage, Paris, the same firm
that created embroidery for Schiaparelli.

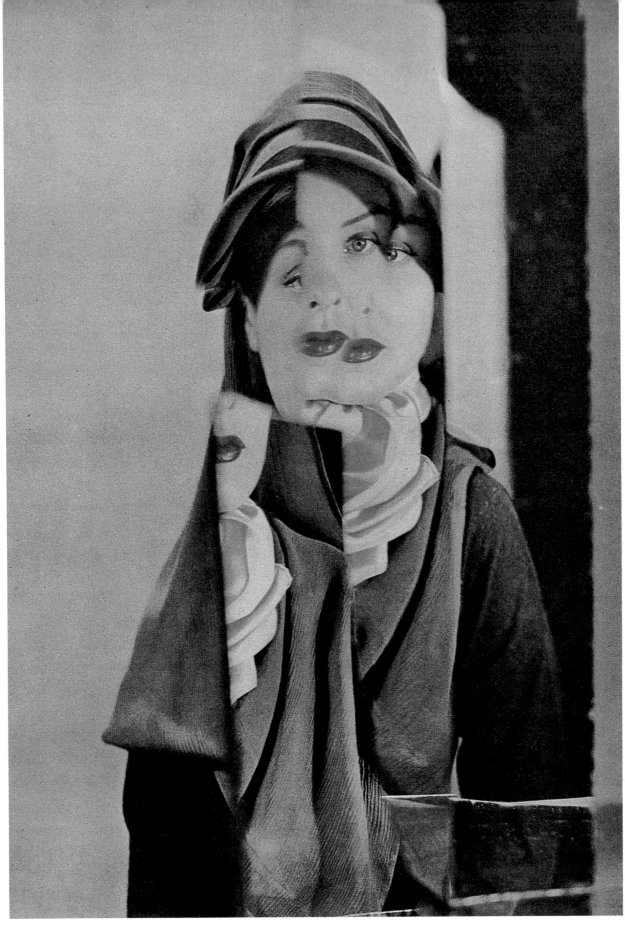

ABOVE
ERWIN BLUMENFELD (American,
born Germany, 1897–1969)
John Frederics Hat, 1947
Photograph

Multiple reflective images together function as
fashion's fractured and exploratory image. The
camera substantiates the elusiveness of
perceptual reality as well as the many mirrors
thereof.

OPPOSITE
HORST P. HORST
Fashion Photograph, 1930s

Horst's photograph of shattered glass reflecting
a young girl is a counterpart of the fractured
glass mirroring beauty in the jackets of
Schiaparelli and Saint Laurent.

ABOVE
CECIL BEATON (British, 1904–1980)
Fashion Photograph, 1938
Courtesy Sotheby's, London

Framed and radiant behind a scrim, Beaton's
model carries her own frame, like a medieval
saint depicted with the sign of her beatitude.

OPPOSITE
HORST P. HORST (American, born
Germany 1906)
Fashion Photograph, 1938
Published Vogue, New York, June 15, 1938

Horst's photographic trompe l'oeil fabricates
and complicates all the circumstances of the
image as it moves from perception to deception,
real to Surreal.

LEFT
RENE MAGRITTE
The Human Condition, I, 1934
Oil on canvas, 39⅛ × 31½ in.
Private collection

To counter the traditional notion that art is the simulacrum of nature, Magritte offered a vexing inquiry into the continuity and simultaneity of nature and art. As one's tendency to read the image as real is subverted, the new reading of the image must be other than real, despite appearances.

BELOW
RENE MAGRITTE
Not to Be Reproduced (Portrait of Edward James), 1937
Oil on canvas, 31⅛ × 25¾ in.
Museum Boymans–van Beuningen, Rotterdam

Dogmatic in title, enigmatic in meaning, Surrealist artist Magritte's portrait with an accompanying volume of Edgar Allen Poe eludes the conventions of mirror and representation.

DOMINIQUE LACOUSTILLE
Window Dress, 1985

Photographed next to the real thing, designer
Lacoustille's witty dress realizes the Surrealist
metaphor. As a window conceals as well as
reveals, so the garment conceals and reveals the
body, affirming the visual congruity of window
and dress.

vertés

"Mirror, Mirror on my suit—"
Schiaparelli

BELOW
RENE MAGRITTE
The Magic Mirror, 1928–29
Oil on canvas, 29 x 21 ½ in.
Private collection

The magic of the mirror resided for the
Surrealists in its similarity to and distinction
from observed phenomena. This mirror of
vanity is the *corps humain*, the human body, its
reflection becoming the very thing to which it
gives an image.

LEFT
MARCEL VERTES (French, born Hungary,
1895–1961)
Jacket with Hand-Mirror Closings, by Elsa
Schiaparelli, 1938
Ink and watercolor
Published *Harper's Bazaar*, New York, April
1938

The paradoxical and discomforting aspect of
the Schiaparelli gesture is that the mirrors
reflected the vanity not only of the wearer but
also of the spectator. As images of the wearer
joined those from the external world, the effect
achieved was like that of Surrealist photographic trompe l'oeil.

ANDRE KERTESZ (American, born
Hungary, 1894–1985)
Distortion #86, 1933
Photograph
Courtesy Edwynn Houk Gallery, Chicago

A suite of nudes, Surrealist photographer
Kertész's Distortion series had two main
objectives: to explore the erotics of
transformation and to develop the aesthetics of
body manipulation.

BODIES AND PARTS

KANSAI YAMAMOTO (Japanese, born
1944)
Advertisement, 1985
Published *Vogue*, Paris, October 1985

An ambiguous form midway between sculpture
and human figure, the organic body emerges
from a rock complete with headdress.

OPPOSITE
JANET NOYCE (British)
Hats
Photograph Iain McKell
Published *The Face*, January 1982

The Surrealist striving for an analogue to the human body
found fulfillment in the mannequin and dress form as well as
in classical statuary. These comparable sets of bodies afforded possibilities for both fashion and the fine arts to represent the figure and to demonstrate the transmutation into
art of the form found in nature. Thus Surrealist poet and
filmmaker Jean Cocteau, in his film *The Blood of a Poet*
(1930), would promote the entanglement between "living
drapery," the classical form that becomes a kind of body, and
the statue, the structure that extends the life of the real body,
setting off a play in transitions between the real and the artificial. Adding theater and lived theatricality to the recipe of a
real world concocted from the ingredients of the imagination,
Cocteau (p. 52), who worked in virtually all the visual arts,
elided the real and the imagined with the same fluidity with
which he moved among the arts. Rejected by doctrinaire Surrealism, Cocteau's film nonetheless called upon Surrealist
styles.

In diverse expressions over the next fifteen years, Cocteau's
obsession with Hellenistic statuary would be played out in
fashion; for example, in 1936 Horst would photograph a
model in fashionable Grecian dress for *Vogue* (p. 51), placing
her against a draped column in an underwater setting; and in
1937 Mme Alix Grès would dress a statuarylike mannequin
in an elegant drapery for the couture pavilion of the Exposition Internationale in Paris (p. 51). Almost a decade later, the
illustrator A. M. Cassandre would bring the image of living
drapery to its ultimate incarnation (p. 65) by eliminating the
figure entirely.

Inhabiting the mysterious piazzas of Giorgio de Chirico, a
painter deeply admired by the first-generation Surrealists,
were mannequins derived from fashion. In *The Disquieting
Muses* (1917; p. 60), they are fitted with hat blocks for heads
(the one on the right having been removed like a hat and set
on the ground as if in respite). In the artist's Metaphysical
landscapes, the figures are standard-bearers for the human,
but their forms do not call to mind images of the Hellenistic
ideal but rather, as William Rubin has pointed out, figures
"made of 'stuff' . . . cloth, wood, metal, cardboard, as well as
other materials."

The diminutive mannequin forming the bottle for Elsa
Schiaparelli's fragrance Shocking (p. 203) is likewise a
standard for the human, but in this case it represents an actual body: that of movie star Mae West, whose hourglass figure was once favored by women of fashion. In a 1938
advertisement, the bottle is metamorphosed into a dress form

49

JEAN COCTEAU (French, 1889–1963)
The Blood of a Poet, 1930
Film Still

In this image from Cocteau's first film, a
calcified Lee Miller plays a figure in transition
between Hellenistic sculpture and real life. The
immobile, stonelike aspect of the body
envisions both the persistence of an artistic ideal
and the anticipation of death.

OPPOSITE ABOVE
Mannequin in Lamé Evening Dress,
by Alix Grès, Pavillon d'Elégance,
Exposition Internationale, Paris, 1937
Photograph Wols
Published *Harper's Bazaar*, New York,
September 15, 1937

Tableaux featuring pitted, statuarylike
mannequins were used for the presentation of
couture fashion at the exhibition.

OPPOSITE BELOW
HORST P. HORST (German, born 1906)
Fashion Photograph, 1936
Published *Vogue*, New York, March 15, 1936

Wearing an elegant Madeleine Vionnet gown,
the model is placed in an underwater grotto
against a classical drapery form. The fantasy
landscape isolates the figure and associates the
dress with both classical garments and the idyll
of the sea.

(p. 62), but the addition of a heart alludes to a living body, bringing the transmutation of forms full circle. Schiaparelli, in her autobiography *Shocking Life* (1954) dwells on the determination of the perfect mannequin from the calibration of West's measurements, thereby fostering the mythos of the figure that becomes the mannequin and the Surrealist ideal of the transference between the living and the inanimate. Surrealism also offered an archaic twist on the identification of the real and less than real. The wandering women of Paul Delvaux's painting *The Staircase* (1948; p. 60) were, like Mae West, Edwardian recollections dressed to historicist standards rather than contemporary taste. The ideal Surrealist woman was unattainable for any number of reasons, but in this rendering of Delvaux's imagination, it was primarily because she was of another vintage, a woman placed in the past never to be wholly retrieved or realized in the present. The juxtaposition of figure and dress form serves as counterpart to the artist's Dance of Death motif in other paintings, where a living figure confronts a skeleton. That the symbol is a dress form and not a skeleton implies a living other and not necessarily death. Thus, the spiritual and living equivalence may be found in the fashion form. Similarly, Man Ray's *Aviary* (1919; p. 72) employs a dress form in place of the living figure and makes the formal armature of the body a place of sanctuary or a cage, the figure eviscerated.

A suite of mannequins were presented as *apparitions d'êtres-objets* (phantom object-beings) by a group of artists at the Galerie Beaux-Arts in the 1938 *Exposition Internationale du Surréalisme* in Paris (pp. 58–59). The last major Surrealist exhibition before the Second World War, it was organized by Paul Eluard, André Breton, and Marcel Duchamp, with the participation of all the major Surrealist artists in France. Related works such as Salvador Dali's *Rainy Taxi* (1938) pressed mannequins into service as char-

acters in a charade—a dormant and provocative masquerade—but the core of the effort was the bizarre collection of mannequins positioned along appropriate city thoroughfares, each figure demonstrating the essential traits of its artist-creator and the possibilities for invention within a given structure. These surrogates for living figures were inevitably subjected to greater distortion and display than living models and perhaps were even more imaginatively dressed than conventional representation would allow. Live models were also used in the exhibition, however, creating real uncertainty as to which were alive and which were not. That these works were achieved in 1938, when many of the Surrealists had embraced disciplines related to fashion suggests the possibility that Surrealism envisioned fashion phenomena as the experience of art and that art had the attributes of fashion. Had the same demonstration of virtuoso talent been presented as a magazine article or a window display, it might have been denied the outrageous and memorable impact of this exhibition in 1938. At the 1937 Exposition Internationale in Paris, the Pavillon d'Elégance had, in fact, already presented mannequins in a manner to engage Surrealist duplicity regarding objects and the real (pp. 51, 56).

The appropriation of mannequins into art in 1938 had specifically been anticipated earlier in the decade by artist-poet Marcel Jean and others. Jean's *Horoscope* (1937; p. 72), which also appeared in the 1938 Surrealist exhibition, used a painted dressmaker's dummy to establish the connection between the living figure and the form in fashion. Herbert Bayer's *Self-Portrait* (1930; p. 66) saw the photographer as a mannequin being disassembled on the spot.

The proposition of Surrealist art as a simulacrum of either sculpture or dressmaking allowed the art a particularly perverse twist on the associations between the artificial and the real. Pygmalion was meeting Freud in a dramatic encounter.

The result was a remarkable analysis of the probity of clothing and its relation to the naked figure. Dali's *Night and Day Clothes of the Body* (1936; p. 69) provided a metaphor for undress and dress. Magritte's *Homage to Mack Sennett* (1934; p. 75) offered the dream and reality of clothing in canny anticipation of a famous advertising slogan, which, beginning in 1949, proclaimed: "I dreamed I was...in my Maidenform bra," and sent the protagonist seminaked into adventures of importance. Magritte established the paradox of clothing as a lesson in body revelation and concealment, the interplay, especially in women's clothing, between the body and its clothing in modesty, but with intimations of the body exposed.

René Magritte admired a brief poem by Paul Eluard: "In the darkest eyes, the brightest eyes have secluded themselves." The Surrealist fascination with the eye, its optical complexity in conscious vision and in unconscious dreaming, sight and voyeurism, blindness and acuity, rendered it as both object to be seen and seeing device. Of the latter, its role in relation to the Freudian tilt of Surrealist interpretation was manifest in Surrealist literature and art, though some artists such as Magritte objected to the purely Freudian interpretation of his optical imagery. Nonetheless, the mutilated eye of *Un Chien Andalou* (1929; p. 79), by Dali and Luis Buñuel would seem to be an unambiguous example of the psychosexual interpretation of autonomous body parts. The eye could achieve independence from the rest of the body and venture into the imagination as both object and subject. Sometimes severed, occasionally Cyclopic, perversely propped up or injured by the presence of a crutch, the eye was both seeing and seen.

The migrations and transmutations of the eye appear in Surrealist objects as diverse as a metronome (Man Ray's *Indestructible Object*, 1923; p. 78), and in garments that bring the eye to the surface (a Schiaparelli dress, providing indispensable testimony to the anthropos of what might otherwise seem to be only a vase of flowers). The Surrealist eye was simulated by Yves Saint Laurent in *Les Yeux d'Elsa* (1980; p. 71), a dress emulating Schiaparelli's style of the 1930s and a tour de force in admiration and advancement of the idea of the eye. Schiaparelli mingled the eye with celestial themes in her Astrology Collection of 1938, a concept also adopted by Larry Shox in his *Celestial Eye Suit* (1985; p. 70). Shox's hybrid suggests the possibilities latent in the eye motif as a Surrealist theme: it is cosmic and at the same time personal and intimate, vision being a shared, world-defining experience of all humans and the specific optic of dreams, both collective and individual. As the eye could be conceived as the representation of a disembodied, derationalized part of the body, its role was both rational in the analytical matters of perception and irrational in the instinctive matters of reverie and imagination. Magritte's *The False Mirror* (1928; p. 78) had, after all, implied the eye to be a representation of the real world, its reality a deeper enigma for its reversal into the self and the "falseness" of the eye being its way of traducing the observed phenomena of the world. If the same dissociated eye is able to transport itself, Horuslike, to the garment, it makes of the apparel a transitional point between the real and reflected, optical and artificial. Indeed, designers such as Schiaparelli and Saint Laurent delight in such a paradox about clothing and use the eye to bring clothing's voyeurism and its spectatorship to the very surface of what Surrealist-inflected fashion might be.

Lovers (1932–34; p. 99), which then became the paradigm for fashion advertisements, with the model placed under the large sign of the lips (p. 85). To establish the lips as the larger and unchanging sign with the variation of figures beneath was essentially to use the Surrealist symbol as a fixed idea.

When lips were liberated, they had the power to migrate to other parts of the body and to serve as the fundamental aperture of the beautiful woman—and conceivably of art itself. As envisioned by Schiaparelli, lips could have their mischievous and erotic aspects; in the Lip Coat (1971; p. 86) by Saint Laurent they might appear to be tamer. That they could be interpretive and suggestive of physical sensuality through symbolic indirection made them a preeminent Surrealist symbol. Furthermore, that Surrealism saw such a symbolic device through transformations in media, level of discourse, changes in decoration, and standards of decorum should serve as an example of Surrealism's latitude with its image-making. The lips of Surrealism give no sign of elitism. Their Surrealist sensuality and symbolism were broadly effective.

Of all the disembodied parts, perhaps the one most vulnerable to fantasy is the hand. Creative yet only obliquely sexual, a composition of parts on its own, functional and essential, the hand provided a protagonist for the Surrealist theater of the body. Perceived as an independent actor visually separated from the body in a photograph by Lee Miller, it could cast shadows in the vision of Maurice Tabard (both 1931; p. 89). It could be observed with clinical clarity, become the evil hand with tapering talons, or serve a useful purpose in closing a garment. The clawlike fingertips and nails of Schiaparelli's Black-Suede Gloves (1938; p. 102) have the sinister charm of the invented and disembodied hand, yet are still recognizably long gloves. The gnarled, withered hands of Dali's apparitional figures in *Woman with a Head of Roses* (1935; p. 90) clutch with the paradox of their utility and their ugliness. For Dali, these grizzled hands can close around the bust or waist, while for a succession of designers the hands provide a natural belting of the waist. Schiaparelli's evening jacket with embroidery by Cocteau (1937; p. 100) benefits from the description of its waist by the hand that holds the cloth, a seemingly natural belt for closing the waist; François Lesage's Hand Belt (1986; p. 101) provides a similar effect; and Marc Jacobs's Trompe l'Oeil Beaded Dress (1986; p. 91), with hands at the waist, is an homage to Schiaparelli. The perambulating hand thus fulfills a function and performs an act we readily associate with its normal utility even while it is sufficiently removed from the body to affirm its independence and to declare its Surrealist volition.

The most voluptuous symbol of Surrealism was lips. From their first appearance in the December 1929 Second Surrealist Manifesto (p. 84) through their long picaresque adventure in the activities of Man Ray, Schiaparelli, Charles James, and Yves Saint Laurent—their contrived dissociation from the figure in the first instance and their placement on a field, resembling a device of ornament in the last—they were both decorative and descriptive. Ironically, Surrealism began with the spoor and only later moved to the lips. The 1929 lips were lipstick traces, signs of the impress of lips, lingering but not entirely palpable shadows of what had existed. The lips of Surrealism become more real even as they became increasingly decorative. Their revisions and reinterpretations—even to the citation of different models for the lips themselves (including Kiki of Montparnasse as one source)—took the form of the Lip Sofa (p. 86) designed by Dali and acquired by Schiaparelli for display in her Place Vendôme boutique; another lip (alternatively identified as a butterfly) sofa by James (p. 147), and the surface decoration of lips on works by Saint Laurent (p. 86) and Hubert de Givenchy (p. 99). Perhaps the prime embodiment was Man Ray's *Observatory Time—The*

Surrealist feet likewise reveal themselves independently and impertinently. They appear as the interior trace on the exterior and a reminder of the corporeality that is Surrealism's foothold. Michel Foucault considers the shoes in *The Red Model* (1935; p. 96) by René Magritte as "resemblance" and "affirmation" in their mutual presence. They travel through Surrealist form and transmutation, from painting to book cover to window display, and back to shoes. The verisimilitude of Pierre Cardin's men's shoes (1986; p. 97) may be lacking in the models by Anne-Marie Beretta and Manolo Blahnik (both 1982; p. 104), but their debt to Magritte is as real. The painting of apparel came first, but fashion followed in art's footsteps.

ISSEY MIYAKE (Japanese, born 1938)
Draped Gowns, 1984
Photograph Scott Heiser

Depicting drapery in such a manner as to
appear wet, Miyake creates a Hellenistic
sculpture of the torso and freezes the movement
of the flying folds.

THIERRY MUGLER (French, born 1948)
Gilded Accessories, 1984
Photograph Roxanne Lowit

Classical drapery and its reference to a
Hellenistic past is transferred from the garment
to accessories, where they take wing on a flight
of fantasy.

SALVADOR DALI (Spanish, born 1904)
Shades of Night Descending, 1931
Oil on canvas, 24 x 19 ¾ in.
Collection Mr. and Mrs. A. Reynolds Morse on
loan to the Salvador Dali Museum, Saint
Petersburg, Florida

Within the mysterious space of the barren
Surrealist plain, a phantom drapery takes on a
living form.

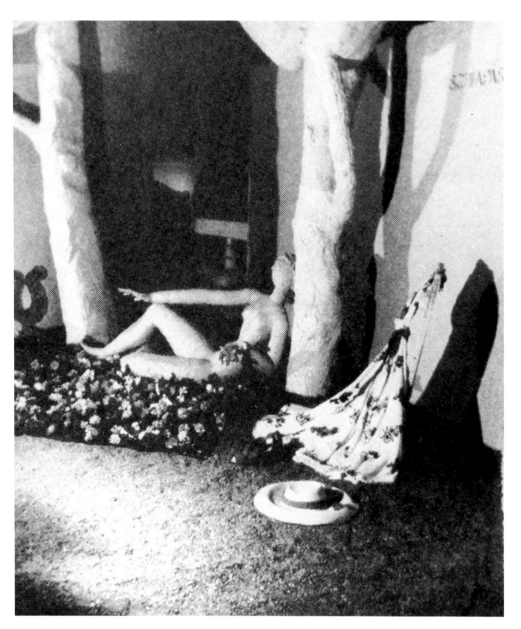

LEFT
Nude Mannequin Partially Covered with
Flowers, by Elsa Schiaparelli, Pavillon
d'Elégance, Exposition Internationale, Paris,
1937
Photograph Wols
Published *Harper's Bazaar*, New York,
September 15, 1937

Schiaparelli's tableau caught public attention
at the exhibition; she placed the nude figure on
the ground and hung an evening dress on a
nearby line. A guest left a calling card with the
mannequin expressing condolences.

OPPOSITE
MAN RAY (American, 1890–1976)
Coat Stand, 1920
Photograph
Published as *Dadaphoto* in *New York Dada*,
1921

Man Ray's *Coat Stand* "stands in" for the
living figure behind it. Moreover, the coat's role
as outerwear is subverted by the complete
absence of dress. Man Ray, in large measure
responsible for the Surrealist passion for
photography, published the single issue of *New
York Dada* in collaboration with Marcel
Duchamp.

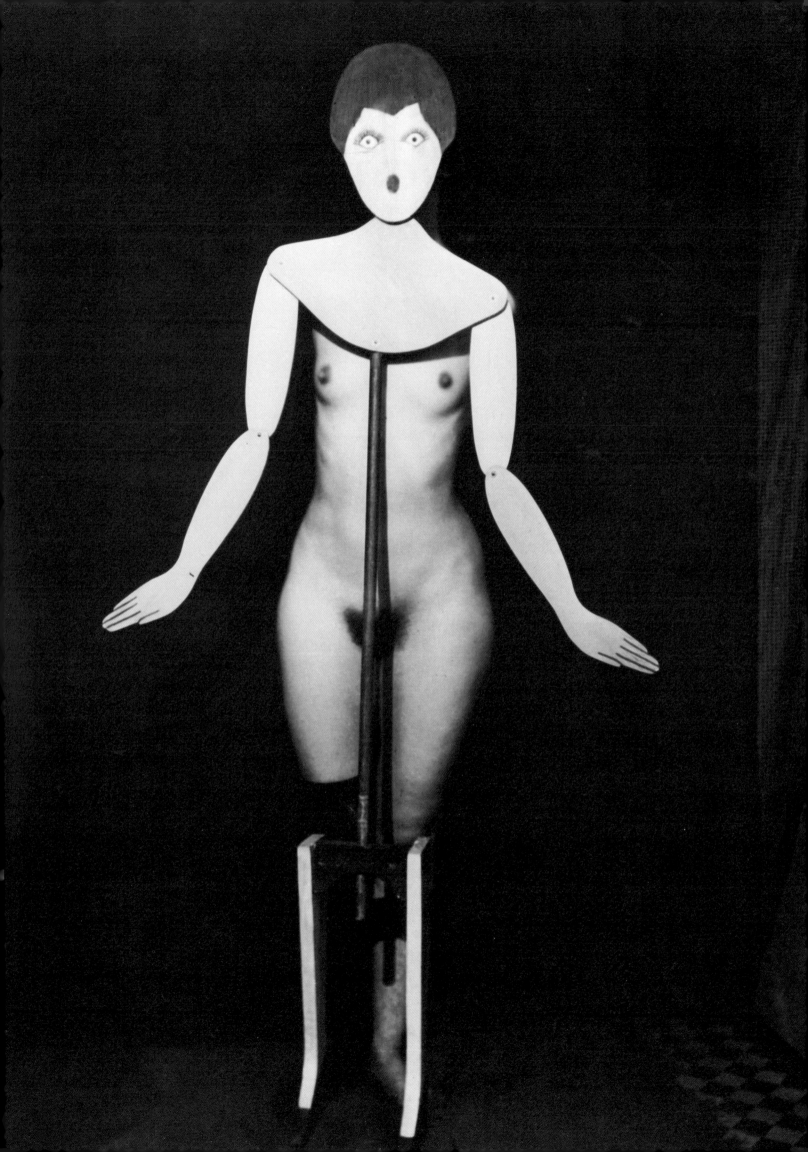

Three Mannequins from the *Exposition Internationale du Surréalisme*, Galerie Beaux-Arts, Paris, 1938
Photographs Man Ray Archives, Paris

Surrealist street lined with mannequins dressed by artists Man Ray, Salvador Dali, Leo Malet, and others (see also p. 193) led to the rooms where the exhibition took place.

OPPOSITE
GABRIELLA GIANDELLI
(Italian, born 1963)
LORENZO MATOTTI
(Italian, born 1954)
Fashion Editorial
Published *Vanity*, Milan, November–December
1986

Giandelli and Matotti collaborated in this
evocation of the de Chirico mannequin,
substituting architectural elements for the
human form. The head is topstitched in a
manner similar to that of a de Chirico model.

RIGHT
JORGE SILVETTI (American, born
Argentina 1942)
Mannequins, Portantina,
New York, 1986
Photograph Paul Warchol

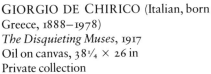

GIORGIO DE CHIRICO (Italian, born
Greece, 1888–1978)
The Disquieting Muses, 1917
Oil on canvas, 38¼ × 26 in
Private collection

The altered dress form is a metaphor combining
mechanistic and personal elements to create a
symbol of the human. Like a puppet, the
mannequin clearly refers to the figure, and the
assemblage of parts is a mechanical equivalent
to anatomy.

PAUL DELVAUX (Belgian, born 1897)
The Staircase, 1948
Oil on panel
Yokohama City Museum

As in the 1930s Mae West in Victorian clothing
was Schiaparelli's paladin of beauty, so Delvaux
dressed his ideal visions in period costume a
decade later. The alternative pure vision is the
dress form at left, offering the inanimate or the
historical.

Shocking de Schiaparelli

PARFUM POUDRE ROUGE A LEVRES MADE IN FRANCE

ABOVE
Advertisement for Shocking, by Elsa
Schiaparelli, 1938
Published *Harper's Bazaar*, New York,
November 1938
Acknowledging the provocative form of

Schiaparelli's flacon for her perfume Shocking,
the artist made the allusion more pronounced
by pinning a heart in the right place on the
bottle-figure-dress form. Film actress Mae West
served as model for the bottle's hourglass
shape.

OPPOSITE
ALFA CASTALDI (Italian, born 1926)
Jacket by Silvano Malta
Published *Vanity*, Milan, October 1984

The aggressive, imaginative dress form in this
fashion-editorial presentation plays with the
body's geometry.

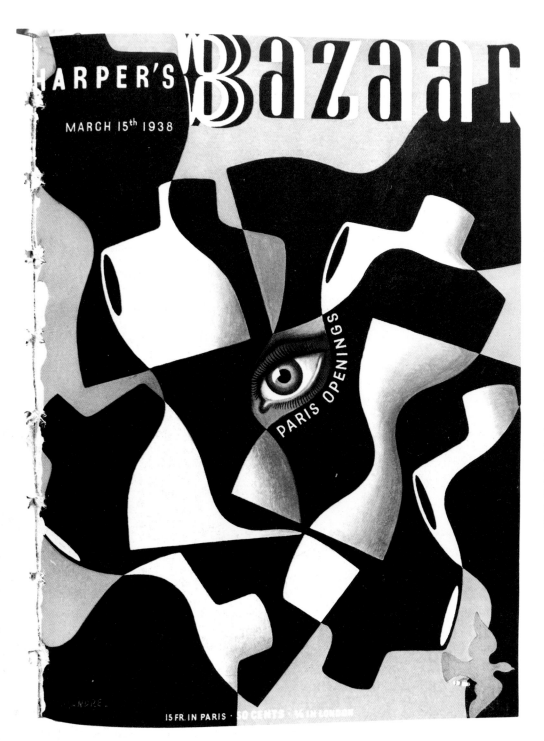

A. M. CASSANDRE (French, born the
Ukraine, 1901–1968)
Paris Openings, 1938
Cover for *Harper's Bazaar*, New York,
March 15, 1938

The inherent abstraction of the dress form is
made manifest through the play of light and
dark and assembly of forms in Cassandre's
design. The Surrealist eye peers through the
keyhole formed by their conjunction.

A. M. CASSANDRE
Advertisement for Lesur
Published 1946

Even without the presence of a figure, the
animation of the drapery suggests a living form,
a classical apparition within the Surrealist
landscape.

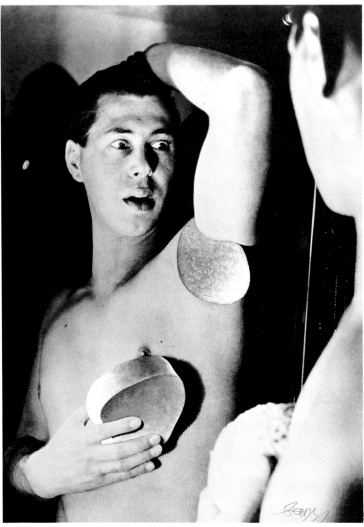

LEFT
HERBERT BAYER (American, born
Germany, 1900–1985)
Self-Portrait, 1930
Photograph
Collection Drs. William and Martha Heineman
Pieper, Chicago

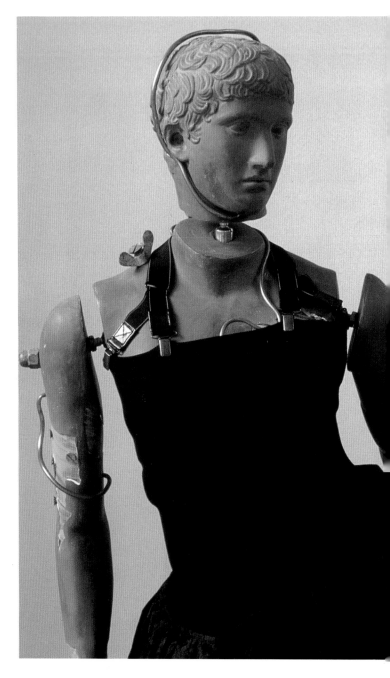

ABOVE
MEL ODOM (American, born 1950)
Men's Shirts, 1981
Published *Playboy Fashion Guides*, Chicago,
Spring–Summer 1981

Converging in Odom's drawing are the
mechanomorph, the mannequin, and the world
of the Apollo Belvedere.

ABOVE
JEAN-PAUL GAULTIER (French, born
1952)
Mannequin, 1986
Photograph François Halard
Published *The World of Interiors*, London, May
1986

Synthesizing classical beauty with the
mechanical and technical aspects of the
mannequin's functional anatomy, Gaultier
exaggerates the androgyny of the classical ideal
by the clothing he selects to attire the
mannequin.

ANTONIO (American, born Puerto Rico, 1943–1987)
Woman's Ensemble, by Gianni Versace, 1981
Published *Vogue*, Milan, 1981

Antonio's disarming mechanomorph bears a striking resemblance to Bayer's *Self-Portrait* (opposite) of some fifty years before.

MARISOL (Venezuelan, born France 1930)
Body Coat (painted on a design by Jacques
Kaplan), 1960
Photograph Taishi Hirokawa
The Metropolitan Museum of Art, New York
The Costume Institute. Gift of Pascal Kaplan,
Ph.D.
Photograph Taishi Hirokawa

Audaciously feigning nudity through the coat,
Marisol recapitulates the concept of Man Ray's
Coat Stand (p. 57).

JEAN-PAUL GAULTIER
Velvet Conical Bust Top, 1984
Photograph Roxanne Lowit

Gaultier's fascination with the bust is a playful
erogeny as well as an analytical view of
structure. His conical constructions of the
breast show his delight in anatomy but also in
the history of style, reflecting tastes of the
1950s.

SALVADOR DALI
Night and Day Clothes of the Body, 1936
Gouache, 11 3/16 x 15 3/4 in.
Private collection

Dali's ingenious antipodes of night and day,
revelation and concealment, stiffness and
softness, and light and dark give form to the
concept of clothing as possessing its own life.
The mystery that Dali offers is the essential
paradox of clothing.

OPPOSITE
YVES SAINT LAURENT (French, born
Algeria 1936)
Les Yeux d'Elsa, 1980
Photograph Claus Ohm

Borrowing a title from Surrealist poet Louis
Aragon and paying homage to Elsa
Schiaparelli, Saint Laurent's caprice honors
words and eyes as Surrealist conventions and
Schiaparelli as the great transmitter of
Surrealist invention to the world of fashion.

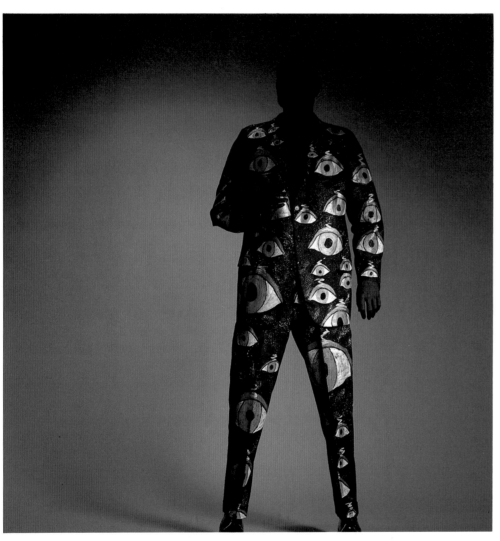

TOP
CLAUDE CAHUN (French)
Object, 1936
Mixed media, 5½ × 6¹¹⁄₁₆ × 3⅞ in.
Courtesy Zabriskie Gallery, New York

The *Exposition Surréaliste d'Objets* at the
Galerie Charles Ratton, Paris, in 1936, included
this displaced eye, which moves about in all-
seeing autonomy from the body, a Cyclops that
finds itself in unexpected places.

CENTER
LARRY SHOX (American, born 1951)
Celestial Eye Suit, 1985
Fashion Institute of Technology, New York
Edward C. Blum Design Laboratory
Photograph Taishi Hirokawa

The eye proliferates and is externalized on this
hand-painted suit. An inner label reads: "Eye
can see."

BOTTOM
SALVADOR DALI
The Eye of Time, 1949
Watch with diamond and cabochon rubies
Minami Art Museum, Tokyo

Understanding more than the flexibility of time,
Dali, the artist of soft watches, considers the
abstractness and the palpable "sense" of time.
He offers time as a dimension and time as a
sixth sense, but he also affirms that time is
never seen except through abstractions.

MARCEL JEAN (French, born 1900)
The Horoscope, 1937
Painted dressmaker's dummy with plaster
ornaments and watch, 28 in. high
Morton G. Neumann Family Collection,
Chicago

Photograph Michael Tropea

Although Man Ray explored the internal
structure of the dress form, Jean restored its role
in reproducing the anatomy, suggesting in his
map that the world is neither round nor flat but
composed of an oddly familiar terrain.

ABOVE
MAN RAY
Aviary, 1919
Aerograph and tempera on cardboard
Private collection

Man Ray views the dress form as part figure,
part bird cage.

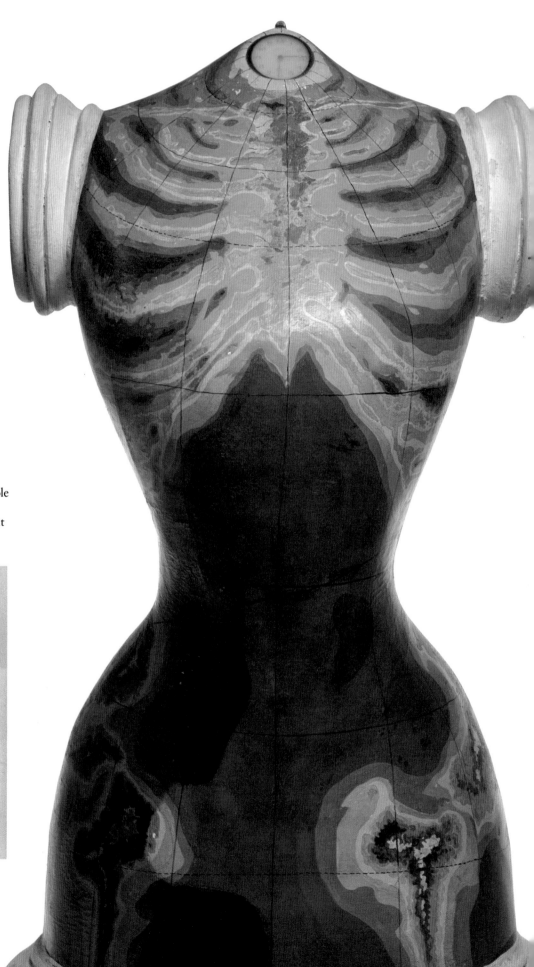

ANDRÉ BRETON

QU'EST-CE QUE LE SURRÉALISME?

RENÉ HENRIQUEZ, Editeur
Rue d'Edimbourg, 13, BRUXELLES

ABOVE

RENE MAGRITTE

Cover for André Breton's *Qu'est-ce que le Surréalisme?* (What Is Surrealism?), 1934
The Art Institute of Chicago
The Mary Reynolds Collection, Ryerson Library

The body is transformed into a face in this classic image of Surrealist enterprise, combining unresolved misogyny and obsession with women.

RIGHT

SALVADOR DALI

Invitation to Dali Exhibition, Julien Levy Gallery, New York, 1936–37
Courtesy Zabriskie Gallery, New York

Dali's fascination with the body is a matter of fetishism, most especially in his breast obsession.

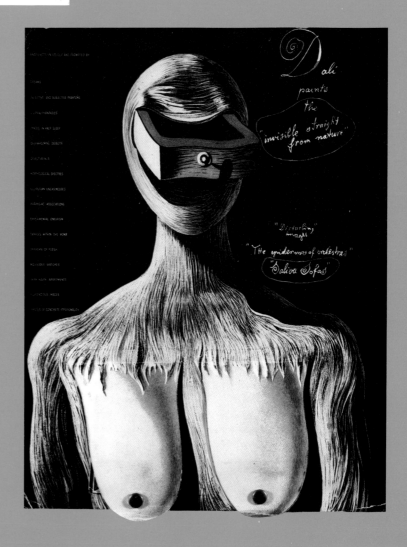

GEORGE PLATT LYNES (American, 1907–1965)
Elizabeth Gibbons with Umbrella and Mask, c. 1940
Photograph
Courtesy Robert Miller Gallery, New York

The scrimlike transparency of the garment, more cocoon than clothing, softens the figure to an elegant nudity while the mask and umbrella accompany such idealism with prurient mischief.

RENE MAGRITTE (Belgian, 1898–1967)
Homage to Mack Sennett, 1934
Oil on canvas, 28¾ × 21½ in.
Musée Communal, La Louvière, Belgium

Magritte explores the intimate eroticism of clothing and the undeniable sense of the individual within the garment. Both the memory of the body and the anticipation of its presence obtain even as the clothing may hang in a wardrobe.

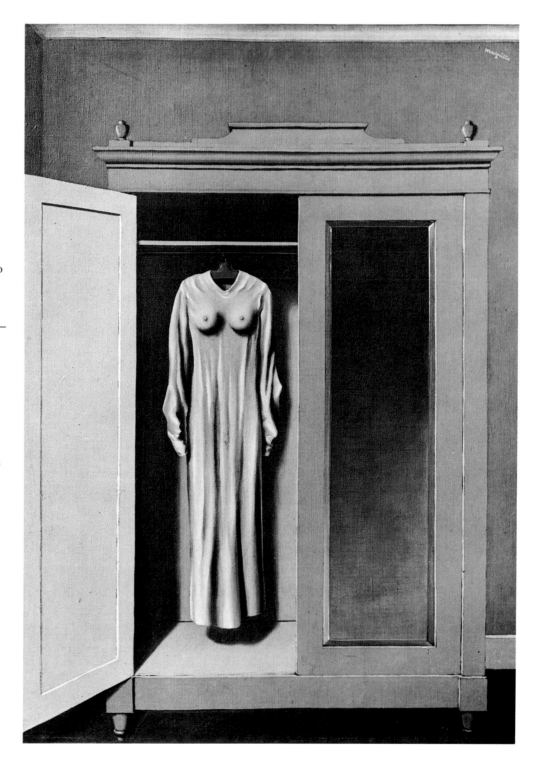

PRIÈRE
DE
TOUCHER

LE SURRÉALISME EN 1947

LEFT
HANS BELLMER (German, born Poland, 1902–1975)
The Top, 1938
Painted bronze, 13 in. high
Collection Joseph and Jory Shapiro, Chicago

Bellmer's voyeuristic sculpture revolves around the artist's fascination with breasts. So clustered, they enjoy an equation with fruit and convey the artist's fascination with his subject even when it is separated from the torso. A classical prototype, the Diana of Ephesus, is evoked.

Je suis toute nue en dessous

Ben

OPPOSITE
MARCEL DUCHAMP (American, born
France, 1887–1968)
ENRICO DONATI (American, born Italy
1909)
Prière de Toucher (Please Touch), 1947
Collage of foam rubber and velvet on
cardboard, 9½ × 8¼ × 1¼ in.
Courtesy Zabriskie Gallery, New York

Duchamp and Donati's erotically charged
design for the catalog of the exhibition *Le
Surréalisme en 1947* alludes to the book's cover
as skin—leatherbound. The media are mixed:
"falsies" are used as the breasts in an edition of
999, the last few of which had to be drawn in
when the supply of foam rubber ran out.

ABOVE
JEAN-CHARLES DE CASTELBAJAC
(French, born Morocco 1950)
Cruciform Dress, 1984

Created by the designer in collaboration with
Conceptual artist Ben [Vautier], the dress serves
as a speaking expression of its contents,
stripping even as it conceals.

RIGHT
YVES SAINT LAURENT
Evening Dress with Gold Body Sculpture by
Claude Lalanne, 1969

Lalanne replicates the soft nude form in hard
metal, giving solid form to flesh. Reviving the
tradition of the breastplate, commonly worn by
men in the ancient world, he creates a
contemporary version in patent disparity with
the soft evening wear with which it is paired.

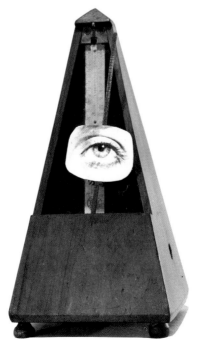

RIGHT
MAN RAY
Indestructible Object (or.*Object To Be
Destroyed*), 1923 (replica 1964)
Metronome with cutout photograph of eye,
8⅞ × 4⅜ × 4⅝ in.
The Museum of Modern Art, New York, James
Thrall Soby Fund

Like Dali, Man Ray offers the conjunction of
time and seeing. The regular intervals by which
the metronome marks time are perceived
through the passage of the eye, a blink that
becomes a moving interval of time.

ABOVE
RENE MAGRITTE
The False Mirror, 1928
Oil on canvas, 21¼ × 31⅞ in.
The Museum of Modern Art, New York
Purchase

Perhaps the most familiar and most
characteristic Surrealist painting of the eye, *The
False Mirror*, acquired by the New York
museum at the time of its exhibition *Fantastic
Art, Dada, Surrealism* in 1936, expands the
optic to a broad vista and floats the pupil as a
void centered in deep space. Understanding all
optical experience to be insufficient without
cognitive or subconscious phenomena in its
support, the Surrealist view as expressed by
Magritte was deeply discriminating and
penetrating.

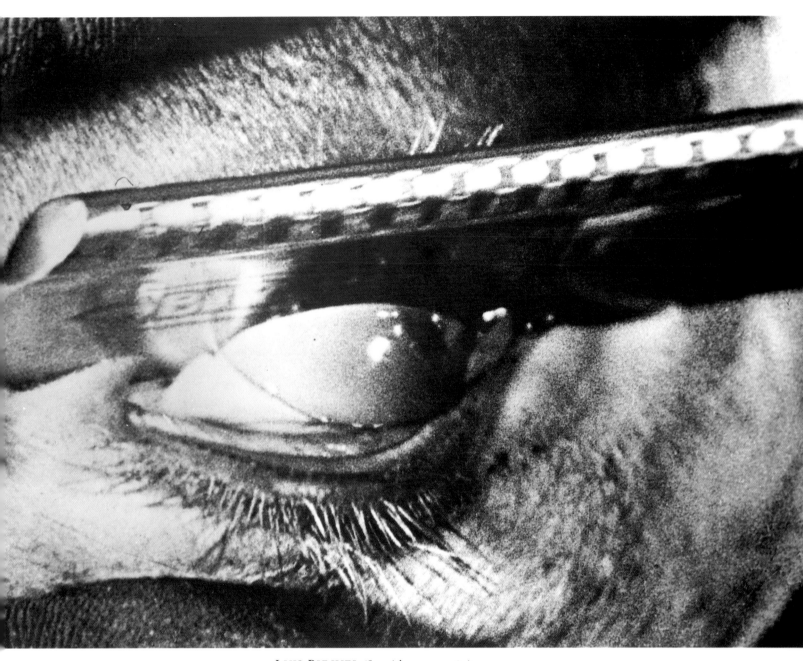

LUIS BUNUEL (Spanish, 1900–1983)
SALVADOR DALI
Un Chien Andalou, 1929
The Museum of Modern Art, New York
Film Stills Archive

Buñuel's and Dali's violent image suggests the
essential role of seeing and the visceral response
to the cutting of an eye.

ABOVE
TONY VIRAMONTES (American, born 1956)
Fashion Editorial: Rifat Ozbek, 1986
Published *The Face*, June 1986

Through photocollage, Viramontes cuts an enlarged Surrealist eye into a hat worn at a rakish angle to obscure the real eye. Thus, the metaphorical eye intrudes vision even as it is vision's symbol.

OPPOSITE
GEORGE PLATT LYNES
Mythology Series: Cyclops, Man with Eye and Wood, 1937–39
Photograph
Courtesy Robert Miller Gallery, New York

Seeking the resonance of mythology in contemporary life, Platt Lynes explored photographic distortion as a means to mythic presence in the most ordinary circumstances.

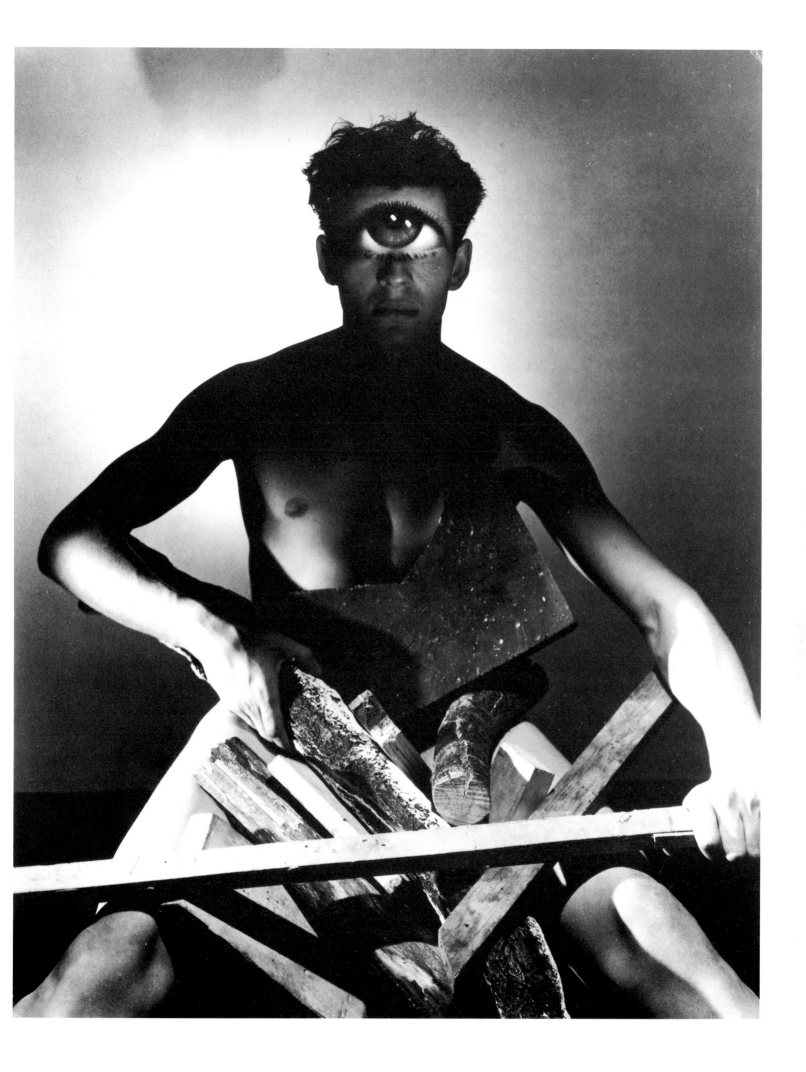

ENRICO DONATI
Evil Eye, 1946
Mixed media
Courtesy Zabriskie Gallery, New York

Donati's refracted vision of the eye as object
took form in a work created for the *Exposition
Internationale du Surréalisme* at the Galerie
Maeght, Paris, in 1947.

GENE MOORE (American, born 1910)
Three Window Displays, Bonwit Teller, New
York, 1952

Realizing the window as optic, Moore created
scenes within the pupil of the eye, a tour de
force based on the Surrealist fascination with
the eye as viewer and vista.

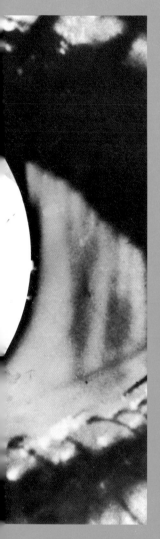
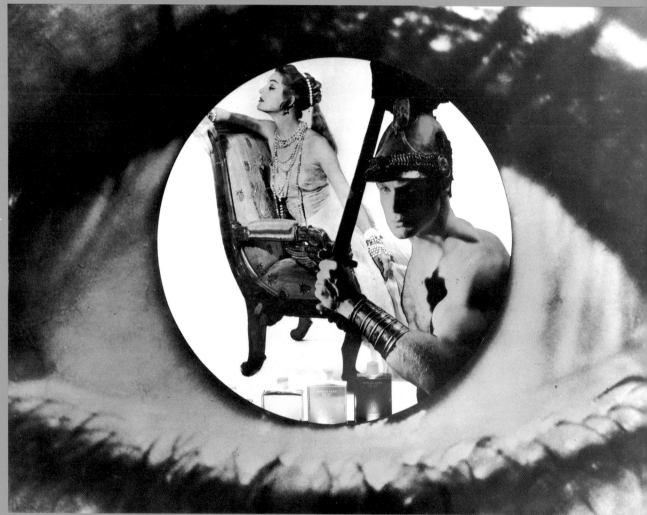

SECOND MANIFESTE DU SURRÉALISME

En dépit des démarches particulières à chacun de ceux qui s'en sont réclamés ou s'en réclament, on finira bien par accorder que le surréalisme ne tendit à rien tant qu'à provoquer, au point de vue intellectuel et moral, une *crise de conscience* de l'espèce la plus générale et la plus grave et que l'obtention ou la non-obtention de ce résultat peut seule décider de sa réussite ou de son échec historique.

Au point de vue intellectuel il s'agissait, il s'agit encore d'éprouver par tous les moyens et de faire reconnaître à tout prix le caractère factice des vieilles antinomies destinées hypocritement à prévenir toute agitation insolite de la part de l'homme, ne serait-ce qu'en lui donnant une idée indigente de ses moyens, qu'en le défiant d'échapper dans une mesure valable à la contrainte universelle. L'épouvantail de la mort, les cafés-chantants de l'au-delà, le naufrage de la plus belle raison dans le sommeil, l'écrasant rideau de l'avenir, les tours de Babel, les miroirs d'inconsistance, l'infranchissable mur d'argent éclaboussé de cervelle, ces images trop saisissantes de la catastrophe humaine ne sont peut-être que des images. Tout porte à croire qu'il existe un certain point de l'esprit d'où la vie et la mort, le réel et l'imaginaire, le passé et le futur,

le communicable et l'incommunicable, le haut et le bas cessent d'être perçus contradictoirement. Or, c'est en vain qu'on chercherait à l'activité surréaliste un autre mobile que l'espoir de détermination de ce point. On voit assez par là combien il serait absurde de lui prêter un sens uniquement destructeur, ou constructeur ; le point dont il est question est *a fortiori* celui où la construction et la destruction cessent de pouvoir être brandies l'une contre l'autre. Il est clair, aussi, que le surréalisme n'est pas intéressé à tenir grand compte de ce qui se produit à côté de lui sous prétexte d'art, voire d'anti-art, de philosophie ou d'anti-philosophie, en un mot de tout ce qui n'a pas pour fin l'anéantissement de l'être en un brillant, intérieur et aveugle, qui ne soit pas plus l'âme de la glace que celle du feu. Que pourraient bien attendre de l'expérience surréaliste ceux qui gardent quelque souci de la place qu'ils occuperont *dans le monde?* En ce lieu mental d'où l'on ne peut plus entreprendre que pour soi-même une périlleuse mais, pensons-nous, une suprême reconnaissance, il ne saurait être question non plus d'attacher la moindre importance aux pas de ceux qui arrivent ou aux pas de ceux qui sortent, ces pas se produisant dans

LEFT

ANDRE BRETON (French, 1896–1966)
Second Surrealist Manifesto, 1929
Published *La Révolution Surréaliste*, Paris,
December 1929

The impress of lips on this crucial document of Surrealist ideology gives literal expression to the body in Surrealist parlance. This frottage initiated a succession of lips in various media.

ABOVE

SALVADOR DALI
Lip Brooch, 1949
Gold with rubies and pearls
Minami Art Museum, Tokyo

Dali added Surrealist lips to the trite compliment of teeth like pearls.

LEFT

VALENTINE HUGO (French, 1890–1968)
Des Gueules (Three Gold Mouths, Two and One), 1934
Oil on wood
Private collection, Paris

To lips made even more erotically charged by their Surrealist displacement to the erogenous zones, Hugo added the sensuality of gold.

ABOVE
MAN RAY
Observatory Time—Venus, 1935–38
Photograph
Man Ray Archives, Paris

BELOW
MAN RAY
Observatory Time—Mode, 1936
Photograph
Man Ray Archives, Paris
Published *Harper's Bazaar*, 1936

Using his painting *Observatory Time—The Lovers* (p. 99) as a background, Man Ray photographed a reclining figure in a Jacques Fath gown in an imitation and interpretation of the painting. Indeed the suite of photographs became Man Ray's reaction to and evaluation of his own painting.

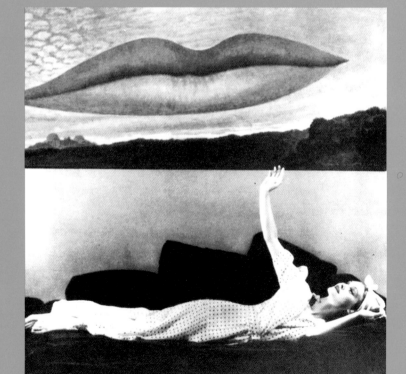

ABOVE
MAN RAY
Lip Necklace
Collection Robert Lee Morris, New York

ABOVE
YVES SAINT LAURENT
Lip Dress, 1966
Photograph Claus Ohm

Seized by Saint Laurent for the bodice of his dress in a manner suggesting Pop art as well as Surrealism, the lips align with the breasts in traditional Surrealist provocation and sexual innuendo.

OPPOSITE
HORST P. HORST
Photograph for Cartier's, New York, 1938

One seeing eye, one hand, and one disembodied head join the other elements of modernist autonomy, rectilinear structure, and tabletop in a fashion study rendering accessories as the primary focus of the photograph.

ABOVE
YVES SAINT LAURENT
Sequined Lip Coat, 1971

RIGHT
SALVADOR DALI
Lip Sofa, c. 1937
Published "Why Don't You . . . " Column,
Harper's Bazaar, New York, April 1938

Lips become three-dimensional in Dali's sofa, an extravagant transformation of the love seat. Elsa Schiaparelli's Place Vendôme boutique in Paris featured the Dali lip sofa in "shocking pink," attracting much attention. The model, however, wears Vionnet for languorous seduction "when you are dining alone with your husband," according to Diana Vreeland in her column.

ART KANE (American, born 1925)
Fashion Photograph, 1960s
Courtesy the photographer

A touch of Michelangelo animates Kane's photograph; the figure floats and hands reach, suggesting fashion to be an intangible, almost ungraspable ideal.

ABOVE RIGHT
LEE MILLER (American, 1907?–1977)
Hand, 1931
Photograph
The Art Institute of Chicago
The Julien Levy Collection, Gift of Jean and Julien Levy

Although the hand would logically remain with the body, the forearm and hand visually seem to be independent, their striving reach, akin to that of symbolic partial figures of modern sculpture, seeming to suggest an emotion focused in one portion of the body. The spiritualist innervation of specific body parts was a mystical source of inspiration for some Surrealists; a hand in expressive grasp may achieve a like effect.

BELOW RIGHT
MAURICE TABARD (French, 1897–1984)
Composition, 1931
Photograph
Courtesy Lucien Treillard, Paris

The altered photograph has its counterpart in the altered body, whereby the hand of the photograph, either literally or figuratively, assumes a role in the depiction. Manipulation is literally the imposition of the hand.

SALVADOR DALI
Woman with a Head of Roses, 1935
Oil on canvas, 13¾ × 10⅝ in.
Kunsthaus, Zürich

The hands wrapped around Dali's figures are
both embracing and twisting, and their
connotation is both erotic and deadly. They
signify erotic engagement as well as physical
restriction and constriction.

MARC JACOBS (American, born 1963)
Trompe l'Oeil Beaded Dress, 1986
Photograph Josef Astor

The designer, who elsewhere acknowledges his
admiration of Schiaparelli, offers an illusion,
and the photographer's use of hands in light
and dark extends the legerdemain.

RENE MAGRITTE
The Titanic Days, 1928
Oil on canvas, 45⅝ x 31⅞ in.
Private collection, Brussels

Superimposed on the body with a figural
credibility by outline, but in apparent discord
with the figure in narrative and specific
description, the male attacks the female in a
struggle made horrific by the merging of the
two figures in an ineluctable union of invasion
and molestation.

YVES SAINT LAURENT
"Pop Art" Dress, 1966

Like Magritte's invasion of the body by
another form, Saint Laurent's dress shares the
form of the wearer with another figure seen in
silhouette. Thus the fictive figure is ever at odds
with the form of the garment suggesting
discomforts of body and veracity.

GEORGE HOYNINGEN-HUENE
(American, born Russia, 1900–1968)
Fashion Photograph, 1938
Published *Harper's Bazaar*, New York,
September 15, 1938

Gold claws extend the fingernails into the
animal vestiges implied in Schiaparelli's
articulated gloves (p. 102).

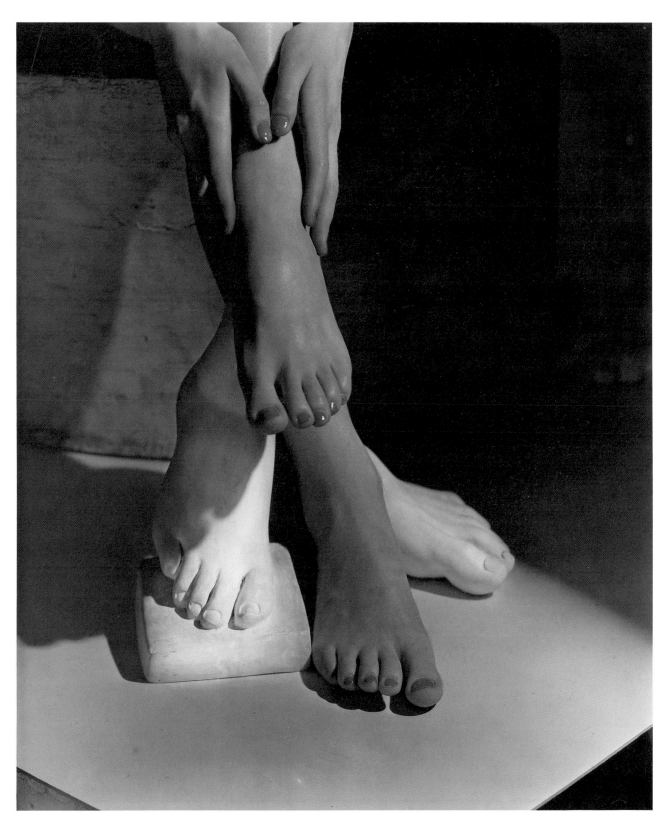

HORST P. HORST
Fashion Photograph, late 1930s

Combining the extremities of classical statuary
with real feet, Horst grants them independence
from the rest of the body in a manner most
unseemly.

OPPOSITE
ART KANE
Men's Trousers by Basile, 1981
Photograph
Published *Uomo Harper's Bazaar*, Milan,
December 1981

Gender invasion and inversion enhance the
allure of Basile's slacks.

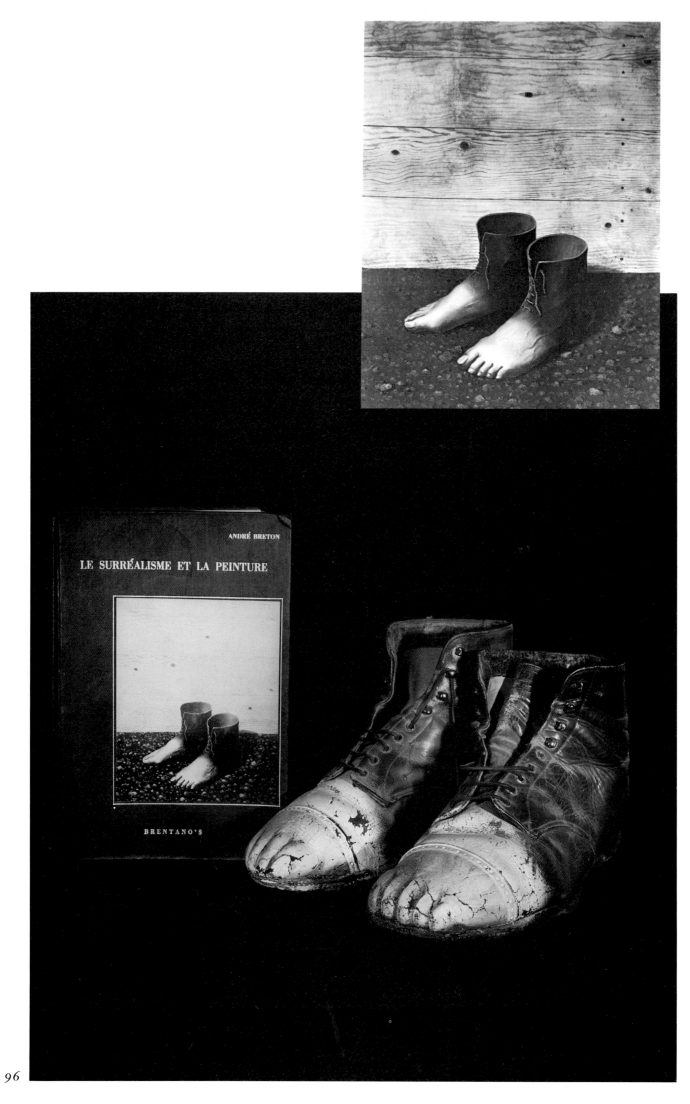

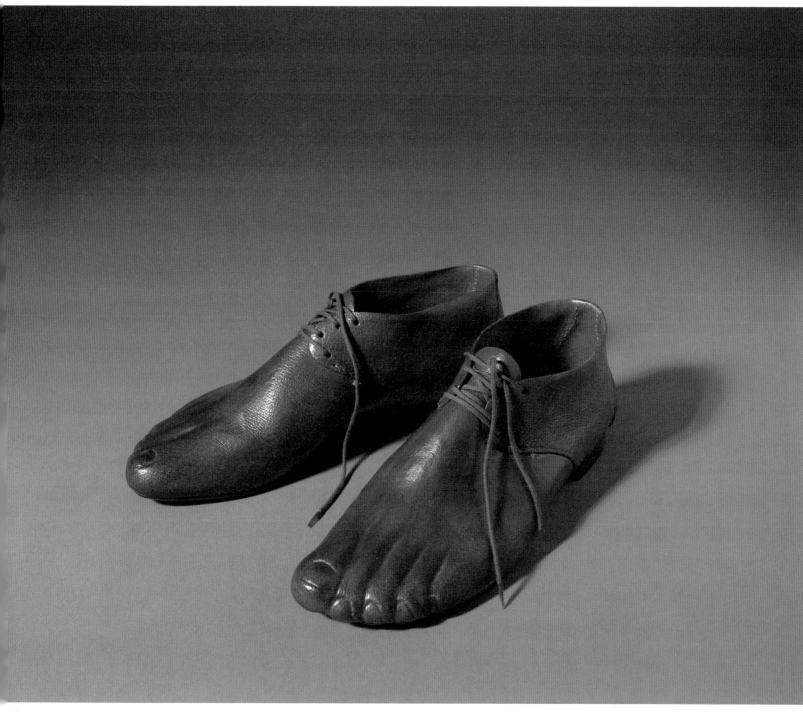

OPPOSITE TOP
RENE MAGRITTE
The Red Model, 1935
Oil on canvas, 21¹⁵⁄₁₆ × 18¾ in.
Musée National d'Art Moderne, Paris

OPPOSITE BOTTOM
MARCEL DUCHAMP
ENRICO DONATI
Window Display, Brentano's, New York, 1945
Courtesy Zabriskie Gallery, New York

Magritte's *The Red Model* itself became a
model through its use as a cover for the second
edition of André Breton's *Le Surréalisme et la
Peinture*. In 1945 Duchamp and Donati
collaborated on a window display promoting
the book at Brentano's, the New York
bookstore. They reproduced the shoes in
emulation of Magritte.

ABOVE
PIERRE CARDIN (French, born Italy 1922)
Men's Shoes, 1986
Fashion Institute of Technology, New York
Edward C. Blum Design Laboratory. Gift of
Richard Martin
Photograph Irving Solero

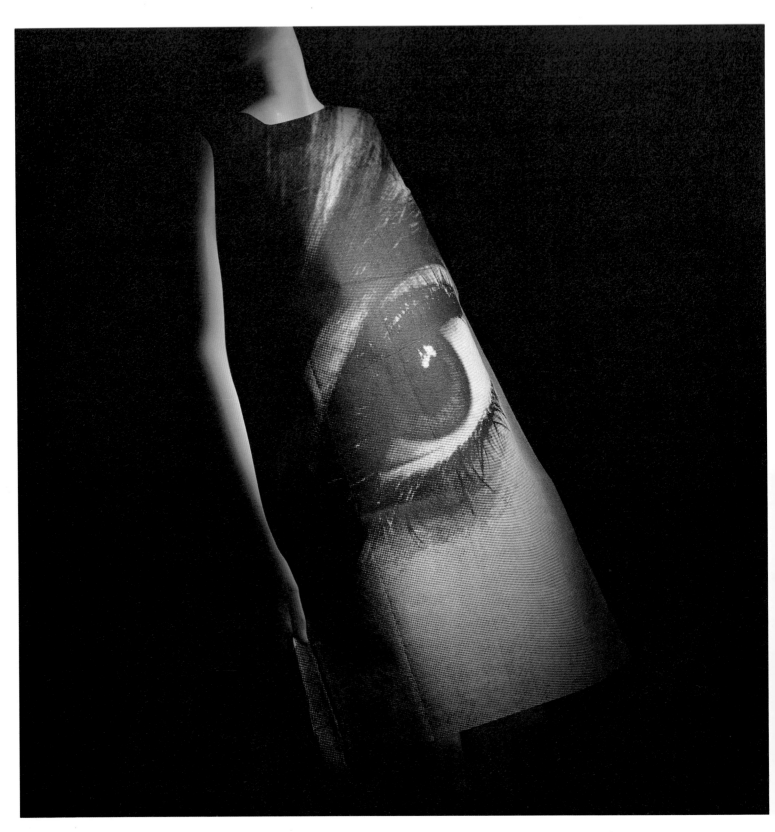

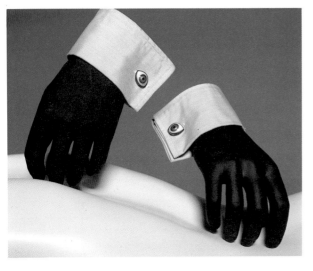

ABOVE
Poster Dress, 1966–68
Fashion Institute of Technology, New York
Edward C. Blum Design Laboratory. Gift of
Stephen de Pietri
Photograph Taishi Hirokawa
A paper dress of the 1960s gives all-seeing
power to the eye.

LEFT
TOM BINNS (British, born 1951)
Eye Cufflinks, 1986
Photograph Taishi Hirokawa

A matched pair, but displaced to the wrists, the
eyes of Binn's jewelry peek mysteriously from
the cuffs.

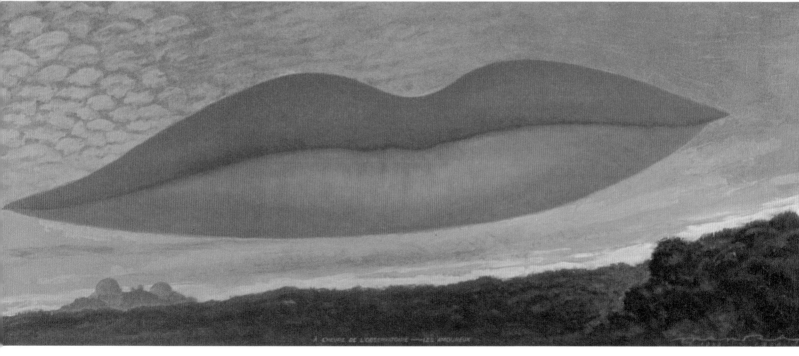

MARCEL JEAN
The Specter of the Gardenia, 1936 (replica 1972)
Plaster covered with cloth, zippers, and strip of film, 10½ in. high
Morton G. Neumann Family Collection, Chicago

Zippers, relatively new in clothing in the 1930s and pioneered by Schiaparelli, close the unseeing eyes of Jean's object. The appropriation for art of a device for advanced clothing separates *The Specter of the Gardenia* from Jean's world-view *Horoscope* (p. 72), an adaption of the old-fashioned dress form.

HUBERT DE GIVENCHY (French, born 1927)
Lip Jacket, 1979

Merging decorative needs with the traditional imagery of the lips, in the 1970s Givenchy adopted the frottage caress on the garment as it had initially been impressed on the page of the Second Surrealist Manifesto.

MAN RAY
Observatory Time—The Lovers, 1932–34 (replica 1964)
Oil on canvas, 39 × 99 in.
Man Ray Archives, Paris

Realizing lips not only as a part of anatomy but as synecdoche, Man Ray visualized lovers in repose as the upper and lower lips.

ELSA SCHIAPARELLI
Jacket with Jean Cocteau Embroidery, 1937
Philadelphia Museum of Art. Gift of Elsa
Schiaparelli
Photograph Taishi Hirokawa

Based on a Cocteau drawing—even including
the artist's signature—Schiaparelli's illusion of
hands clasping the waist is complemented by
the placing of the full profile of a figure and a
cascade of hair down the arm. Schiaparelli
creates discord between the fictive figure and
the wearer, frustrating our attempt to place the
parts of the body in direct relationship to the
figure in the torso but providing accurate
placement of the waist.

FRANÇOIS LESAGE (French, born 1929)
Hand Belt, 1986

The Lesage sleight of hand has long been
employed by various designers for embroidery,
but he brings his virtuoso illusion to a belt of
his own design, in which hands clasp the waist
as if in confirmation of the belt's tightening of
the body. In the 1980s, the House of Lesage
was expanded, not only creating embroidery
for the couture but also crafting its own
production. It now shares retail quarters on the
Place Vendôme in Paris with Schiaparelli.

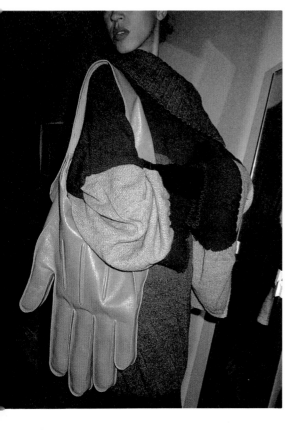

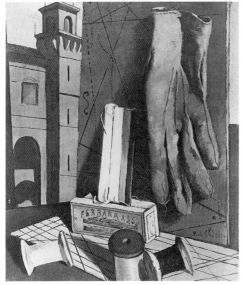

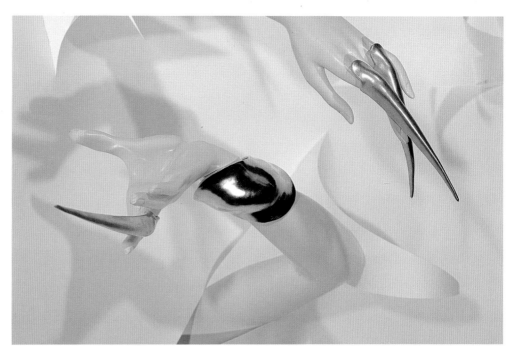

OPPOSITE TOP LEFT
JEAN-CHARLES DE CASTELBAJAC
Glove Bag, 1984
Photograph Roxanne Lowit

The glove as metaphor for the hand and the
literalization of a hand bag affiliate the hand
with fashion: it plays the role of accessory in
the Castelbajac and perhaps serves the young
girl in sewing in the de Chirico.

OPPOSITE BOTTOM LEFT
GIORGIO DE CHIRICO
Amusements of a Young Girl, 1916
Oil on canvas, 18¾ x 16 in.
The Museum of Modern Art, New York
James Thrall Soby Bequest

OPPOSITE TOP RIGHT
ELSA SCHIAPARELLI
Wrist-Length Black-Suede Gloves with Red
Snakeskin Nails, 1938
Philadelphia Museum of Art. Gift of Elsa
Schiaparelli
Photograph Taishi Hirokawa

When the glove both articulates and modifies
the hand, the relation between the perceived
hand and the hand underneath can be sinister
and elegant. When the articulation is subverted
by the materials and colors of the glove,
however, resemblance and discrepancy are
amplified.

OPPOSITE BOTTOM RIGHT
ROBERT LEE MORRIS (American, born
Germany 1947)
Fingers, 1980–81
Photograph Taishi Hirokawa

RIGHT
THIERRY MUGLER
Metal Fingertips, 1986
Photograph Michel Arnaud
Published *Vogue*, London, April 1986

As so much was present in the fascinating
interstices between the conscious and
subconscious for the Surrealist imagination, so,
too, much was evocative in the interval between
the primitive and human. When Mugler's
golden fingertips appeared in 1986, British
Vogue called them "the ultimate gesture."

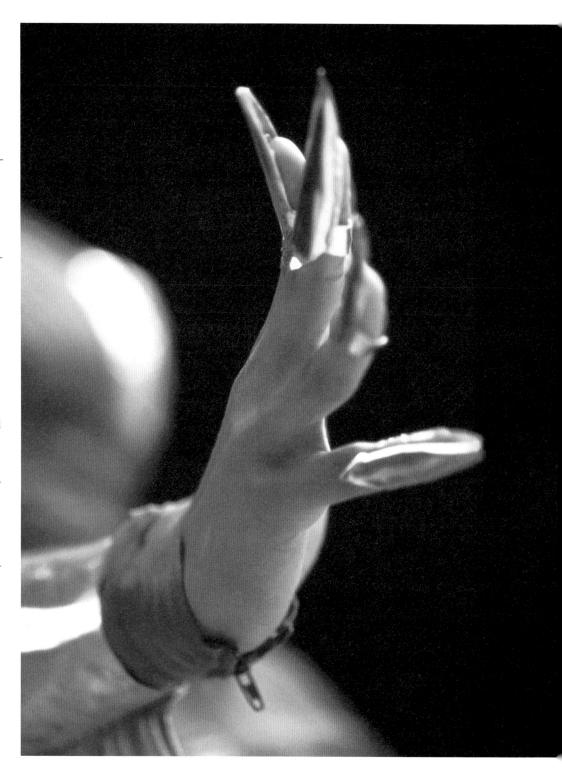

ABOVE
ANNE-MARIE BERETTA (French, born 1937)
Toe Sandal, 1982
Photograph Roxanne Lowit

Deriving their irony from Magritte (p. 96), subsequent versions of feet-shoes sustain a long iconography, if seldom a practical style.

ABOVE RIGHT
MANOLO BLAHNIK (Spanish, born 1943)
Sketch for the Glove Shoes, 1982

Blahnik creates a hand and foot metaphor and massage.

BELOW RIGHT
MANOLO BLAHNIK
Magritte "Siamese Twin" Shoe, 1982
Published *Vanity*, Milan, April 1982

Rendering homage to Magritte, Blahnik considers the transposition into a practical and extravagantly aesthetic shoe. The foot slips into one-half the shoe and carries thereby the full boot.

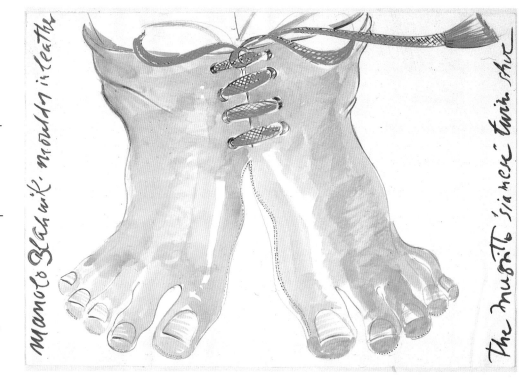

JOAN MIRO
Object, 1936
Mixed media, 31⅞ × 11⅞ × 10¼ in.
The Museum of Modern Art, New York
Gift of Mr. and Mrs. Pierre Matisse

Out of a hat emerges a lyric fantasy with a fetish object composed of a suspended high-heeled shoe. Derived in part from Dali's *Object of Symbolic Function* (1931), which gave like primacy to a high-heeled shoe, Miró's *Object* is anomalous within his oeuvre as an object construction, but it is consonant with his obsession with the transmuted body.

l'Acacia

la Lune

la Neige

le Plafond

l'Orage

le Désert

Magritte

DISPLACEMENTS AND ILLUSIONS

The Surrealist object was essentially an exercise in displacement. Like the bottlerack Marcel Duchamp bought at a Paris bazaar in 1914 and inscribed, the Surrealist object became art as a function of its dysfunction and displacement. Altered by its removal from its conventional milieu, causing disruptions in role, association, and even scale, it shifted identity through its new designation as Surrealist object. Thereafter, it would offer a contradiction between the accustomed recognition and its new definition in art. In the painting *Dreaming's Key* (1930; opposite) by Magritte, displacement similarly plays on the discrepancy between our customary apprehension of an object and its revised context. And in fashion, a hand bag that appears to be a fan or clock can be equally startling (p. 122). Knowledge is placed in jeopardy as the unconscious offers interpretations for objects seen.

The hats of Surrealist fashion have offered some of the most bizarre examples of displacement. Lobsters, pastries, and mutton chops have disported themselves as hats, suggesting the heady folly of the Surrealist enterprise. Whereas most items of dress afford only limited opportunity for the display of seemingly autonomous objects, the hat at the crest of the living figure offers a perfect field. Moreover, the Surrealists joined masqueraders and low comedians in perceiving the antic potential of the silly hat. In its conventional association with ceremony, propriety, and rank, the hat plays a symbolic role. The object replacing the hat or the hat resembling an object thus plays a symbolic role as well, even in the game of diminishing the propriety of the figure. When a miniature chair is placed on the head (as Karl Lagerfeld so elegantly did, see p. 123), one plays not only with the conventions of furniture but also with the humorous dislocation of the entire process of sitting.

Elsa Schiaparelli's Shoe Hat (p. 111), a classic of the genre, brings the foot to the head with the contortionism that delighted the Surrealists. Proposed by Salvador Dali in a sketch and confirmed by Schiaparelli's own drawing (both 1937; pp. 110–11), the Shoe Hat has its antecedents in Surrealist play. During a 1932 visit to Port Lligat, Dali was photographed next to a Surrealist object of obscure meaning and seemingly provisional fabrication (p. 110); he was already playing with the placement and purpose of the straying shoe, for it served as both hat and epaulette for the artist. Eventually Gala Dali was photographed wearing the Dali-Schiaparelli Shoe Hat, by which time the reversal was not only from bottom to top but also from husband to wife: who wears the shoe in a given photograph? The comic irony

OPPOSITE
RENE MAGRITTE (Belgian, 1898–1967)
Dreaming's Key, 1930
Oil on canvas, 32 × 23¾ in.
Private collection

The Surrealist subversion of reasoning is evident in the scramble of names and objects (egg = acacia; shoe = moon; hat = snow; candle = ceiling; glass = storm; hammer = desert). The child's play of learning specific epistemological concepts becomes then a lesson in displacement, a substitution of unconscious and antirational for rational meanings.

with which Dali and Schiaparelli perceived the hat has been pursued by many designers. In the 1980s, Kirsten Woodward and Stephen Jones perched hats as daffy as a tilted ewer and spilling French fries on the head (pp. 117, 125). Hatmakers have also taken license with the conventional materials of hatmaking. Beginning with feathers, they might investigate the special possibilities Surrealism allowed for the noncontextual displacement of the object and its role as an amusement in complement to its being an aesthetic argument. Thus, the feather hat readily becomes a chicken hat— a perched bird—now risible yet beautiful in its transformation into the mere barnyard chicken. Schiaparelli had conceived of such organic millinery in 1937 (p. 113), and Bill Cunningham did the same in the 1950s (p. 125). The swathing of the hat around the head and the word "head" became the field for a suite of heads of lettuce, cabbage, and sundry other greens offered as hats (p. 124). That the displacement is offered in language and meaning as well as in an ironic view of objects certifies the literary and Surrealist cast of these fashion heads. The expressive anti-utility of the redefined object serves fashion as a powerful force, just as it did the art of the twentieth century. But if the Surrealist ambition to marvel at the mundane is to be attained, perhaps art is not necessarily its sole medium; rather, the displacement that fashion allows in being both mundane and in affording opportunities to be visually and intellectually marvelous is equally important.

The inventive hats of Surrealism top the list of displacements, but other possibilities exist as well. One article of clothing may be substituted for another. Karl Lagerfeld cinches the waist with gloves, a variation on the concept of the separable hand. John Galliano invents the jacket to become pants, and Jean-Charles de Castelbajac animates the skirt as a shirt, again displacing our sense of top and bottom. Historical and usually invisible clothing was made apparent when the corset, reminder of an earlier era, was employed as a bracelet by Paul Flato (1939), as a hat by Lagerfeld (1985–86), and as a dress by Jean-Paul Gaultier (1986; other versions as early as 1982; pp. 115–17). These displacements within the fashion context are perhaps even more effective because the "objects" persist as apparel but alter their specific role or place within the assembly of apparel items. The inebriated partygoer may wear a lampshade on his head, but it is not necessarily a viable hat; the Surrealist wearer with a shoe on her or his head may be more intoxicatingly provocative. Significantly, the item of Surrealist apparel must offer some degree of authenticity. The Schiaparelli Mutton Chop Hat (c. 1937; p. 108) is a millinery fiction, but in order to be fully acceptable it has a white patent-leather frill on the end of the chop as if offered in proper restaurant service. The Pastry Hats (p. 123) designed by Karl Lagerfeld are sufficiently detailed to seem delicious and not merely allusive; they look delectable not deceitful. André Breton once expressed his admiration for Duchamp's disdain of all thesis. It is the same device that Surrealist disorientation of fashion provided: a license to redesign all existing fashion objects and objects external to the figure. The floating, somnambulant world of Surrealist figures allowed for the misalliance of familiar objects and the reevaluation of all objects, especially those which obtained on the body as fashion.

A hat posing as a chair offers the possibility of transference

MARCEL VERTES (French, born Hungary, 1895–1961)
Schiaparelli Mutton Chop Hat, c. 1937
Published *Harper's Bazaar*, New York, January 1938

Delighting in the radical gesture of the mutton chop on the head, Schiaparelli made her hat plausible by her specific and excellent detailing. Her joke is a finesse to an already absurd circumstance, the custom of "dressing" the lamb chop with a paper frill or "panty" at its tip between furniture and apparel, but the prime example of this crossover is the fusion of body as a bureau, of pockets as drawers, and of the vestment as furniture. In its most sinister example, the adornment of a dress could be, with deadly wit, the handle of a casket, as in François Lesage's embroidery (c. 1950; p. 133); but fashion also practiced a slightly less macabre interpretation of the furniture and apparel continuum as well. Dali's concept of the City of Drawers, or the penetration of drawers into the body (a "chest of drawers") was represented not only in his sculpture *Venus de Milo with Drawers* but also in his pencil drawing *Study for Anthropomorphic Cabinet* (both 1936; p. 120). A talismanic image for Dali, the woman as the place of drawers conflated two themes of the artist: woman-as-object and the erotic penetration of the figure. Dali's eroticism and the vanity of the subject were transformed in Schiaparelli's Desk Suit (1936; pp. 118–19). The artistic convention remains the same, but certain stylistic aspects suggest an altered interpretation. Indeed, the woman who wears the suit of drawers has become conventionalized, in that Schiaparelli places this Surrealist invention on a conservative suit, thus promoting its association with furniture and displacing the naked eroticism offered by Dali. More discreet, the Schiaparelli suit offers an uncertain illusionism in that some of the drawers bear the function of pockets and others appear only to simulate the furniture. The designer's fascination with novelty and her choice of utilitarian objects for buttons achieves prominence here, as the drawer pulls and buttons are one and the same. Photographed by Cecil Beaton in a barren landscape suggestive of a Dali painting, the image by a Surrealist artist is modified by a designer and then rendered in a Surrealist mode by its photographer. By this move in and out of explicit Surrealism, the suit holds us in its thrall, even as it seeks some degree of conventional acceptance. The wilder invention is the Painted-Silk Drawer Dress (1984; p. 121) created at the Paris school of fashion Studio Berçot; with its pockets and protuberances overflowing with jewelry, it returns to the eroticism and flamboyance of Dali's original image.

Just as Dali's invention of the woman with drawers had implicated the Venus de Milo, so has much Surrealist invention come from the reinterpretation of classical beauty, endowing that convention with the convulsiveness and dreamlike quality that Surrealism considered appropriate to the artistic state. Classical forms underwent multiple transformations in the Surrealist imagination, and even classical architecture was appropriated by Surrealist designers—in theater and film, as has been demonstrated, as well as in fashion. The canon of classical forms in architecture, most especially the column, was incorporated into all aspects of design. It is said that Schiaparelli called upon the classical column when creating evening masks for galas, using them as the vertical elements by which the masks could be held before the eyes. Whole figures were incorporated into classical architecture, whether by de Chirico in his inventions for the 1929 Ballets Russes production of *Le Bal* (p. 130), where they became living forms not merely of the column but of the classical temple—yet with modern intimations in the brick fabrication of the lower legs and arms—or more recently by Adelle Lutz for David Byrne's film *True Stories* (1986), in which figures also emerge from classical architecture as well as from contemporary brick face (p. 128). Both Man Ray and Hans Bellmer imposed brick face in Surrealist painting, the former in his

MARCEL VERTÈS
Schiaparelli Inkpot Hat, 1938
Published *Harper's Bazaar*, New York,
March 15, 1938

Schiaparelli transforms the thinking cap into the convenience of the writing cap. She offers a quill pen ever ready for inspiration, not the least her own in appropriating objects to millinery.

SALVADOR DALI at Port Lligat, c. 1932
Photograph Gala Dali

As early as 1932, Dali anticipated his future collaboration with Schiaparelli by posing with his wife Gala's slipper on his head. Five years later, this histrionic move would be effected in clothing resembling the actual object.

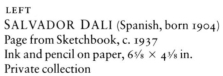

LEFT

SALVADOR DALI (Spanish, born 1904)
Page from Sketchbook, c. 1937
Ink and pencil on paper, 6⅝ × 4⅜ in.
Private collection

Having worn the shoe himself, Dali designed a shoe hat for Schiaparelli around 1937. The heel-over-head, topsy-turvy reversal had become more than a moment's improvisation for the camera, and *Dreaming's Key* became encoded in a stable but provocative object.

ELSA SCHIAPARELLI (French, born Italy,
1890–1973)
Sketch for Shoe Hat, 1937
Musée des Arts de la Mode, Paris
Schiaparelli Studio Sketchbook, U.F.A.C.

MARCEL VERTÈS
Schiaparelli Shoe Hat, 1937
Published *Harper's Bazaar*, New York,
September 15, 1937

The operagoer Vertès depicts may seem *blasé*,
but her astonishing shoe hat would
undoubtedly be startling to others. Schiaparelli
observed the formal similarities between a shoe
and a peaked hat with projecting cone, but
knew that her hat would ever be seen as a shoe
transplanted and transmogrified. The betrayal
of conventional meaning, Surrealism's
revolution, achieves its *tricorne* here.

OPPOSITE
ELSA SCHIAPARELLI
Hen in Nest Hat, 1938
Published *Vogue*, New York, March 15, 1938
Illustration by Eric

Sitting pretty is Schiaparelli's "chicken in a nest" hat. *Vogue* described it as "just for fun" and a "foible," but Schiaparelli's hat alludes to the materials of millinery, combining a straw nest with the feathers of traditional hatmaking. No advocate of animal rights, Schiaparelli nonetheless scored an unforgettable point about the folly of the conventional hat. Her gesture is the Surrealist altering of traditional images to suggest new possibilities.

ABOVE LEFT
MICHAEL ROBERTS (British)
Fashion Photograph, 1985
Published *Tatler*, London, October 1985

ABOVE RIGHT
LANCE STEADLER (American, born 1955)
Fashion Photograph, 1986
Published *Vogue Italia Pelle*, Milan, May–June 1986

Each image puts its best shoe forward, taking Dali's joke into the 1980s. The artistic joke, increasingly commonplace with such revivals of interest in Surrealism as Bruce McLean's paintings and the 1985 film *Brazil*, becomes a conventional epigram of disorientation.

LEFT
VALENTINE HUGO (French, 1890–1968)
Woman with Chicks, 1937
Engraving
Courtesy Jacques Damase, Paris

Whether Hugo realized that the world of engraved fantasy would be made real is uncertain, but its coincidence with the Schiaparelli Hen in Nest Hat suggests that little is stranger than fashion.

Vogue

PARIS OPENINGS II • MARCH 15, 1938 • PRICE 35 CENTS

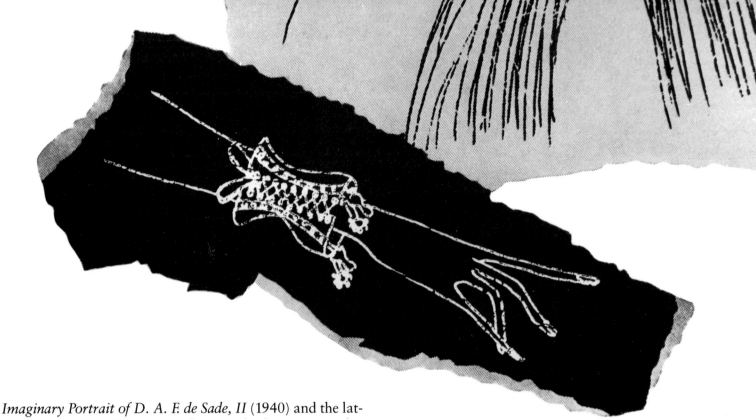

Imaginary Portrait of D. A. F. de Sade, II (1940) and the latter in his *Child and Seeing Hands* (1950; both p. 132). By this literal animation of architecture and the past, the figure becomes architecture in the most arresting way and the flexibility of the figure becomes a construction on the apparent solidity of architecture. Ionic column and Gallé lamp, which seemingly have weight and fixity of place, are given license by the designs of Lutz (p. 129) and Dominique Lacoustille (p. 127) to come to life, as in an animated cartoon.

As clothing offers the illusion of intractable forms made of hard materials and photography and film allow for momentary uncertainty when confronted by living beauty and sculpture of the classical past, so the figures in the pristine plains of Dali's *Three Young Surrealist Women Holding in Their Arms the Skins of an Orchestra* (1936; p. 135) appear to offer some uncertain transition between life and immortality.

In 1937, Dali and Schiaparelli collaborated on what has come to be known as the Tear-Illusion Dress. It featured a cape in which the tears were real and a dress on which the tears were fictive, playing with the integrity of material in much the same way as de Chirico had played with the elements of classical architecture. "Beauty will be convulsive or it will not be," said André Breton. To offer the dress with tears is to recreate the convulsive horror of the first apprehension of beauty. The modernist assumption of rejection can be a premise for fashion as much as any other artistic expression. In this instance, the dialogue between cape and dress makes that friction between the perceived and the cognitive ineluctable. If in the lassitude of some fashion the dress were eventually to dissolve into mere decoration, it could not do so in the presence of its cape, for the two styles support the plausibility of one another. Thus, we must perceive the real tears as much as we must acknowledge their illusion on the dress. Further, the mysticism of penetrating without tearing asunder becomes more viable when it is accompanied by the physical manifestation of the dress without rupture. Dress thereby becomes, as it does in assuming the attributes of furniture, architecture, and sculpture, a resembling and referential art form, not simply a matter of apparel, but a possibility for art and its affinities.

Moved to the wrist and transformed into gold by the alchemy of the Surrealist imagination, the corset no longer serves its initial purpose, which is to constrict and therefore to achieve a fashionably slim waist. Here the normally flexible twentieth-century corset is supplanted by a firm form that falsifies constriction but still achieves the end of showing a fashionably slim wrist.

Of all the inappropriate places for this normally concealed undergarment to perch, the head is perhaps the most improbable, a disjunctive connection perfect for Lagerfeld's style of irony and decorum. Lagerfeld, however, also offers an anachronism along with the movement of the garment to the head. By using an archaic garment, he confirms its movement in time as well as around the body. Further, that he gives external format to an undergarment exposes the devices of structure to external examination. In its several issues of displacement, the Corset Hat functions with the complexity of any Surrealist object.

JEAN-PAUL GAULTIER (French, born 1952)
Corset Dress, 1986
Photograph Roxanne Lowit

Since 1982, Gaultier has made a succession of studies of the corset, turning this traditional undergarment into an external feature of dress, an anticipation of popular-culture adaptation of intimate apparel to external wear.

ABOVE RIGHT
MAN RAY (American, 1890–1976)
Mina Loy, 1918
Man Ray Archives, Paris

The Dada-Surrealist appropriation of vernacular objects extended to adapting them for use as accessories. In this new role, the object hovered between brilliant improvisation and the testing of art's premises, here a cool calculation of a thermometer as an accessory. Jasper Johns's *Thermometer* (1960) might seem to be the inheritor of this immodest earring. Mina Loy, the wife of Arthur Cravan, contributed to the New York Dada periodical *The Blind Man* in its two issues of April and May of 1917 and was part of the Surrealist circle in Paris during the 1930s.

CENTER RIGHT
KIRSTEN WOODWARD (British, born 1960)
Vase Hat, 1986
Photograph Alastair Thain

Wonderfully misappropriated, precariously unbalanced, and cannily tilted in readiness to serve, Woodward's ewer is an empty vessel, but also a perfect topknot transformed into a decorative object; it makes reference to women carrying vessels on their heads, a leaning vase, and the history of classical and neoclassical decorative objects.

BELOW RIGHT
MAN RAY
Meret Oppenheim, c. 1950
Photograph
Man Ray Archives, Paris

For Oppenheim, artist of the *Fur-Lined Teacup* (1936), it was not inappropriate to wear champagne-cork earrings. The motif reappears in Stephen Jones's Dom Perignon millinery and accessories of the 1980s and may have a source in Salvador Dali's *Aphrodisiac Dinner Jacket* (1936), from which there hung an abundance of drinking glasses.

LEFT
ELSA SCHIAPARELLI
Sketch for Desk Suit, 1936
Musée des Arts de la Mode, Paris
Schiaparelli Studio Sketchbooks, U.F.A.C.

OPPOSITE
CECIL BEATON (British, 1904–1980)
Schiaparelli Desk Suit, 1936
Photograph
Courtesy Sotheby's, London

The Schiaparelli Desk Suit may not represent a direct collaboration with Dali, but it is inspired by Dali's concurrent works (see p. 120). The suit, however, is a subdued variation on the theme. It features pulls for the fictive drawers that are ambiguous: some are "real," functioning as pockets, and others are false. Beaton's photograph avowedly places the model in a Surrealist landscape.

OPPOSITE
DOLINE DRITSAS (French, born 1963)
Painted-Silk Drawer Dress, 1984
Photograph Roxanne Lowit

Although Schiaparelli tamed the drawers concept to a suit for the office, Dritsas returned to the libido and lasciviousness of Dali's concept, creating half-painted surfaces and drawers dripping with costume jewelry.

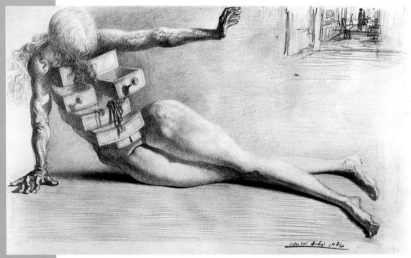

ABOVE
SALVADOR DALI
The City of Drawers: Study for Anthropomorphic Cabinet, 1936
Pencil on paper, 12⅝ × 20½ in.
The Art Institute of Chicago. Gift of Frank B. Hubachek

LEFT
SALVADOR DALI
Venus de Milo with Drawers, 1936 (cast 1964)
Bronze
Private collection

Fraught with anxiety over entry into the body of a woman, Dali offers a series of drawers as possible access. The artist spoke of "kinds of allegories" related to the drawers and the need to smell the "innumerable narcissistic odors emanating from each one." Even the Venus de Milo is subject to such corporeal access.

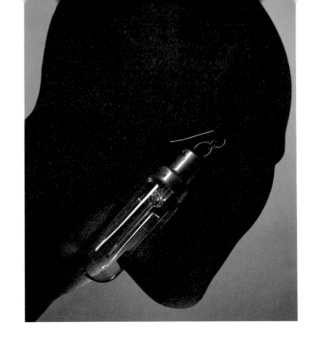

TOM BINNS (British, born 1951)
Electric-Bulb Earring, 1986
Photograph Taishi Hirokawa

A jeweler-artist working in London, Binns
probes the world of pure invention as well as
the history of Surrealism for transposed and
transformed objects. Bent forks and rubber
fishes in kinship with Dali, single mysterious
eyes, and bizarre clocks occur frequently in his
work. In this case, his earring is incandescent
with aesthetic inspiration.

LEFT

LEDERER (founded Vienna, 19th century)
Fan Bag of Gold-Stamped Black Satin
Collection Mark Walsh, New York

Clock Bag of Black Suede, 1950s
Fashion Institute of Technology, New York
Edward C. Blum Design Laboratory

Champagne-Bucket Bag of Black Suede and
Plastic, 1950s
Collection Mark Walsh, New York

Photograph Taishi Hirokawa

Fashion accessories may foster illusions
antithetical to clothing's functions, as in the
three handbags here. A related 1950s telephone
handbag previously attributed to Schiaparelli
and her leek, eggplant, and cauliflower
"vegetarian" bracelet also set clothing's real
function in antithesis to its seeming
identification. The still-life composition of
alternative forms is not unlike Magritte's
arrangement of objects in *Dreaming's Key*.

OPPOSITE ABOVE
KARL LAGERFELD (French, born
Germany 1938)
Pastry Hats, 1984
Photograph Roxanne Lowit

In Lagerfeld's caprice of displacement and
substitution, one can have one's cake and wear
it, too. Like Schiaparelli's 1937 Mutton Chop
Hat, these *patisserie* accessories speak to the
Surrealist imagination of *Dreaming's Key*, in
which a fictive identification of the object is
presented with sufficient declarative force to
seem convincing. No confection, however
delicious in sight or taste, matches the sweet
delight of Surrealist wit.

OPPOSITE BELOW
KARL LAGERFELD
Chair Hat and Upholstered Dress, 1985
Published *Vanity Fair*, New York, September
1985
Photograph Daniel Jouanneau

By wearing a *fauteuil* brooch, a tufted-
ottoman dress, and sitting on a chair matched
to the hat, the model is placed in an even more
incongruous, but strangely sympathetic,
relation to her chair hat.

FROM LEFT
GERMAINE VITTU
Head of Lettuce Hat, 1942
Green silk
The Metropolitan Museum of Art, New York
Gift of Mrs. Alexander P. Morgan

ERIC BRAAGAARD
Salad Hat, c. 1968
Green silk
Fashion Institute of Technology, New York
Edward C. Blum Design Laboratory
Photograph Taishi Hirokawa

EMME (Ethel Price)
Head of Cabbage Hat, 1957
Green silk
The Metropolitan Museum of Art, New York
Gift of Natalie Lieberman

Inasmuch as they are referred to as "heads" of
lettuce and cabbage, these hats establish their
similarity to heads in language as well as in
visual displacement. Like certain other
Surrealist fashions, they provide in clothing a
colloquial affiliation between body and food.
The female as serving tray for foods was a
party specialty developed by Salvador Dali in
his *Dream of Venus*, the pavilion he designed
for the 1939 New York World's Fair.

STEPHEN JONES (British, born 1957)
French Fries Hat, 1984
Colander Hat, 1984

Jones's boldly inventive hats based on
vernacular items are beautifully made, not-for-
one-time-wear creations. Literally madcap in
their inventiveness, they take part in the
tradition of Surrealist objects—ever impudent
and inspired.

ABOVE
LOUISE BOURBON (French?)
Chicory Beret, 1938
Published *Harper's Bazaar*, New York,
December 1938
Photograph Georges Saad

Surrealism's more popular ramifications
involved introducing many everyday items into
the repertoire of millinery. Designer Bourbon
used whatever materials were at hand, from a
funnel to a feather duster to French rolls. In
this case, she worked with chicory—not a
semblance, but the real thing, a festoon from a
legume.

CENTER RIGHT
BILL CUNNINGHAM
(American)
Chicken Hat, 1950s
Photograph Taishi Hirokawa

Cunningham created a marvelously alive and
slightly sinister chicken, but one with pluck.

LEFT
MARINA KILLERY (British, born 1960)
Shortcake Hat of Straw, Satin, and Fake
Strawberries, 1985
Published *Vogue*, London, November 1985
Photograph Paolo Roversi

The British designer concocts a hat to be
carried on the head with the skill of the most
agile waiter.

OPPOSITE
DOMINIQUE LACOUSTILLE (French,
born 1956)
Gallé Lamp Dress, 1980s

A Gallé lamp is now seized from history and
given Pygmalion incarnation in a dress that
illuminates both the decorative arts and
clothing.

OPPOSITE ABOVE AND BELOW
ADELLE LUTZ
Urban Camouflage Clothing, 1986
Photographs Annie Leibovitz
Published *Vanity Fair*, New York,
October 1986

The Ionic Column stands among its architectural confrerès in Lutz's Urban Camouflage costumes for the David Byrne film *True Stories* (1986). It was philosopher Roland Barthes's belief that there is a discrepancy between clothing and the external world, but Lutz seeks to resolve that separation. In publishing the photograph of David Byrne in Lutz's Brick Suit (below), *Vanity Fair* wrote: "If there's any artist Byrne truly resembles in his pallor, his perfected otherness, his powdered aura, it's the writer-director-artist Jean Cocteau."

RIGHT
ADELLE LUTZ
Urban Camouflage: Study for Classical Column, 1986

In simile, the body is often described as a column: in fashion, pleating is said to resemble the fluting of a column. Lutz goes beyond simile to create the garment and column as one and the same.

grey hair w/white streaks.

pale make-up

padded urethafoam

FAUX MARBLE on CHINA

TRUE STORIES "URBAN CAMOUFLAGE"

padded

incorporate fluting into the edge.

flats and flats.

ABOVE AND BELOW LEFT
GIORGIO DE CHIRICO (Italian, born
Greece, 1888–1978)

Le Bal: Woman's Costume, 1929
Pencil, watercolor, and gouache on paper,
10⅞ × 7⅞ in.

Le Bal: Program Design, 1929
Pencil, watercolor, and gouache on paper,
15⅞ × 11 in.

Wadsworth Atheneum, Hartford, Connecticut
From the Serge Lifar Collection, the Ella Gallup
Sumner and Mary Catlin Sumner Collection

The vocabulary of classical architecture
provided the theme for de Chirico's costume
and decor design for *Le Bal*, produced by
Diaghilev's Ballets Russes in 1929 and
choreographed by George Balanchine. De
Chirico's sketch of the Woman's Costume
invites speculation on clothing's role in both
enclosure and disclosure, as well as on the
solidity of classical architecture. The figure
seated in the comfortable armchair (below) is
attired in elements of a classical frieze, but
comic relief is provided by his brick-faced lower
arms and legs, a departure from the
neoclassical theme. Derided by the first-
generation Surrealists for his association with
the ballet, de Chirico retained the faceless
mannequin figures that had appeared in his
work from the teens onward.

SALVADOR DALI
Advertisement for Bryans Stockings, 1946
Published *Vogue*, New York, November 1,
1946

Commerce also builds on the architectural
metaphor in Dali's interpretation of the "bricks
as legs" simulation, a masonry quadrille
contrasting sheer stockings with brick legs. The
comparison of women to architecture ("built"
or "stacked") is a conventional and long-
standing vulgarism.

KRIZIA (Italian company, founded 1954)
Ionic Column Bathing Suit, c. 1982
Illustration by Antonio

HANS BELLMER (German, born Poland, 1902–1975)
Child and Seeing Hands, 1950
Ink and watercolor on paper, 11½ × 9½ in.
Collection Joseph and Jory Shapiro, Chicago

Although Bellmer's brick hands are manifestly a construction of the mind, their mysterious combination of sight and touch bears the suggestion of dungeons and castles and the latent sexual threat they imply.

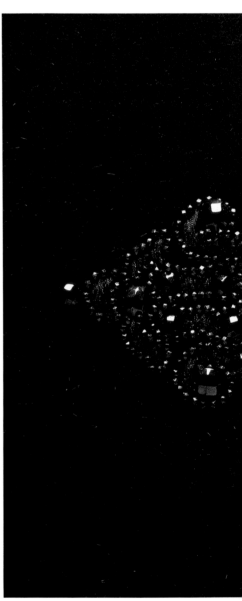

MAN RAY
Imaginary Portrait of D. A. F. de Sade, II, 1940
Oil on canvas, 20 × 16 in.
Private collection

The Marquis de Sade—man, monument, and emblem of Surrealist freedom and rebellion—is seemingly being created from the stones of the Bastille, the notorious Paris prison representing oppression to partisans of the French Revolution. In this, the ambiguity of the Surrealist interpretation of history is evident. While freedom and revolution are extolled, a monument, even a fantasy one, is constructed with the materials of the past detached from one history to be newly encoded in another.

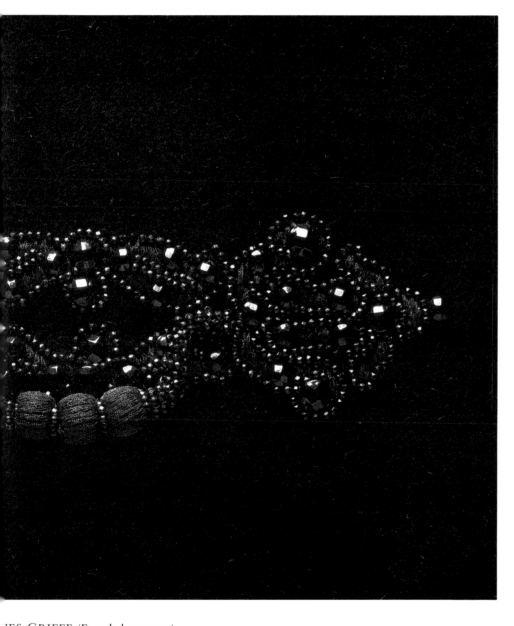

JES GRIFFE (French, born 1917)
Handle Embroidery, c. 1950
dered by Lesage, Paris
aph Taishi Hirokawa

h Dali's drawers were lubricious,
Casket Handle, intended to decorate a
is sinister in its association with a
d the abiding Surrealist premonition

RIGHT
MAGRITTE
ive, 1963
on paper, 14⅛ × 10⅝ in.
seum of Modern Art, New York
Harry Torczyner

MARCEL ROCHAS (French, 1902–1955)
Trompe l'Oeil Jacket, 1930s
Photograph Harry Meerson

Rochas's substitution of solid forms of
architecture for the more pliant forms of the
body creates clothing as a built shelter for the
body.

SALVADOR DALI
*Three Young Surrealist Women Holding in
Their Arms the Skins of an Orchestra*, 1936
Oil on canvas, 21¼ × 25⅝ in.
Morse Charitable Trust, on loan to the
Salvador Dali Museum, Saint Petersburg,
Florida

Flower heads, a limp cello, and a soft piano are the music of this Dali painting. The middle figure wears a "tear" dress, as if in revelation of the body, but in decided contrast to the figure on the left, which seems more radically exposed through its drapery. Moreover, although the middle figure may be said to reflect Dali's collaboration with Schiaparelli on the fabric for the Tear Dress (p. 137), which appeared a year later, it also promotes the illusion that the tears are on the body and that no dress is there whatsoever.

REI KAWAKUBO (Japanese, born 1942?)
Lace Sweater, 1982
Photograph Peter Lindbergh

Like Schiaparelli, Kawakubo only teases the
viewer with the possibility of the torn
garment. Indeed, she respects the
integrity of the material, but offers the illusion
of a defiled garment.

ELSA SCHIAPARELLI
Tear-Illusion Dress and Head Scarf, 1937
Philadelphia Museum of Art
Gift of Elsa Schiaparelli
Photograph Taishi Hirokawa

To tear the dress is to deny its customary
decorum and utility and to question the matter
of concealment and revelation in the garment.
Although the Tear Dress, a collaboration
between Dali and Schiaparelli, is an evening
gown to be worn in the most formal
circumstances, it is presented as if it were in the
most aggressively deteriorated state. At the
time of the Spanish Civil War, when Fascism
was spreading throughout Europe, the
references to shattered glass and rent fabric
must have held strong implications for both the
political and visual worlds. A *memento mori*,
the garment was in a state of destruction even
when it was new. The Dali-Schiaparelli gesture
is extended in torn garments of 1970s and
1980s punk and in high design in Rei
Kawakubo's 1982 "lace" sweater, slashed at its
inception and similarly counterpointing the
objectively perfect and the purposefully
imperfect.

NATURAL AND UN-NATURAL WORLDS

Surrealism navigated strange waters. It was an art of the depths, not only of psychological and intellectual immersion but also of the actual depths of marine and aquatic life. Sirens, fish, and shells entered the worlds of Surrealism and fashion. In a plate from Max Ernst's collage-novel *Une Semaine de Bonté* (1933–34; opposite), shell and head converge in a Surrealist personification of water. One of Chanel's rare Surrealist-inspired designs is a white-grosgrain hat in the form of a shell (1938; p. 157), on which a Surrealist Venus could have been borne up. In the 1930s Surrealist beauty was at its convulsive peak as it plunged into or emerged from water and allowed earthly beauty to commingle with the beauty of the sea. Stylistic extensions of the fish from the title page of *La Révolution Surréaliste* of December 1, 1924 (p. 140) proliferated. The fish inscribed "Surrealism" would swim through decades of imagery.

A strategically placed lobster became an important part of an evening dress designed by Elsa Schiaparelli in collaboration with Salvador Dali in 1937 (p. 146). Represented in *Harper's Bazaar* as *la robe homarde*, the lobster dress partook of many Surrealist motifs of the period. The lobster's prehistoric appearance in contrast with its rather refined association with food—as well as its metamorphosis in color as it goes from sea to table—made it an eminently suitable symbol. Indeed, the Neptune theme had caught the imagination of the Surrealists and their patrons, inspiring a masquerade at the villa of the Comte de Noailles in 1929 (p. 142) and the costume worn by the Comtesse de Noailles at a ball the following year (p. 155). The lobster, however, was the preferred symbol for Dali. Perhaps drawn to the claws, prehensile pincers, feelers, and hard carapace for their resemblance to certain insects, which recurred in his paintings, he may have found that it is the lobster as exemplar of human primitivism that held the greatest attraction. Moreover, the history of the lobster submerges us in aqueous ancestral origins, allowing us to realize a history of development that is not limited to terrestrial life.

For Dali, the lobster could be associated with both the instrument of the telephone and the instrumentality of the fig leaf, the former affiliating the lobster with mouth and ear, the latter with genitalia. The lobster is at once armored and naked. Dali's lobster telephone (1936; p. 145) coyly made the receiver of the telephone (with the mouth and ear combination new in the 1930s) into a point of erogenous and amusing contact. Hand, mouth, and ear were all implicated in the use of the new telephone; Dali understood their nexus

OPPOSITE
MAX ERNST (French, born Germany, 1891–1976)
Plate 4 from *Une Semaine de Bonté*, vol. 2: *Water*, 1933–34
Collage-novel, published Paris, 1934

Ernst's personification of water, a little bit dominatrix, wears a shell hat.

Title page from *La Révolution Surréaliste*, Paris, December 1, 1924

"We are at the eve of a revolution," declared the editors of *La Révolution Surréaliste* in its first issue, and they promised the reader: "You can take part." The visual catch was the Surrealist fish—but also offered were automatic writings and accounts of dreams.

to be as absurd as it was utilitarian. The lobster might also crawl on a Dali head, but most frequently Dali associated the lobster with covering female pudenda, where its role was both menacing and modest. A series of photographs by George Platt Lynes of Dali in the company of a female model with a lobster testify to the discomfort of this imagery (c. 1939; p. 144). Moreover, Dali's 1939 water ballet *The Dream of Venus*, designed for a pavilion at the New York World's Fair, combined the body and seafood in erotic and unsettling juxtapositions. Dali placed a lobster over the body of a live model, encircled another with an eel, and made seafood a necklace and an offering placed in the hands of still another figure. Other Surrealist festivities associated the body with food, but seldom with the clarity of Dali's particular obsession with the lobster.

Thus, as Guillaume Apollinaire had taken a lobster out for a walk on a leash in Paris, so Dali and Schiaparelli took a lobster to the evening dress, making of the Surrealist image something even more elegant and bizarre. The dress places the lobster on a white field flecked with parsley. It is the red lobster, the comestible—not the green-brown underwater live lobster—but its reference to the deep is present nonetheless. The dress serves as counterpart to the model in the George Platt Lynes photographs, for the lobster is covering the genitals in its central position on the front of the dress. Unseemly as dressmaking and conventional behavior, the dress is perhaps even more outrageous and inappropriate than it might at first seem. It alludes to the woman's nudity beneath her clothing and provides a Surrealist sign of sex organs. Dali's inspiration was as wicked as it was winsome and the resulting dress is both a delight and an affront. American designer Charles James created a lobster in dress form (p. 147) that paid decorous homage to Schiaparelli.

The Surrealist vision of marine life has been sustained in contemporary fashion by Cinzia Ruggieri's Dress with Octopus (1984; pp. 148–49) and Adam Kurtzman's Manta Hat (1986; p. 148). More sophisticated is the vision of Yves Saint Laurent. The imbrication of fish scales in his richly sequined Sardine Dress (1983; p. 149) gives the mermaid new life as a slinky siren. René Magritte's *Song of Love* (c. 1950–51; p. 143) transfers a human emotion to fish by means of two strange hybrids in which the attributes of human and fish are completely confused. Fish torsoes meet human legs, as if floundering in a sea of love. The braided cone of Christian Lacroix's Shell Hat (1984–85; p. 156) is both the twisting of cloth and the outline of sea shell.

André Breton had called the automatic pieces he published in the First Surrealist Manifesto (1924) *poisson soluble* (soluble fish). Primitivizing, unspeaking, mysterious, and evocative, the undersea world held its Surrealist fascination.

Of all the sites of the natural world that were favored by the Surrealists, the most mysterious was the forest. With rare exception urban and sophisticated, the Surrealists would seldom have found themselves in anything more dense than a grove, but they depicted the forest as a place of fantasy and adventure, alluding, perhaps, to the primeval forest of the Symbolists. To be sure, an altered reality would seem to have transformed the woods of Magritte's *Discovery* (c. 1928; p. 160) and Ernst's portrait of Caresse Crosby (1932; p. 161), but Paul Delvaux's *Birth of the Day* (1937; p. 161) tames nature and brings its trees and glades to a picturesque and poetic form. In an animistic view, it was possible to see the tree as achieving the form of woman and its natural beauty cast in the female role. Natural and nurturing, the tree-woman serves as a tranquil earth-mother in her leafy beauty. What art imagined, fashion also depicts in Vivienne Westwood's Tree Coat (1986; p. 150) and Cinzia Ruggieri's Weeds Dress (1983; p. 150). What fashion evokes, photography saw in the transmutations of figure and environment, the tree and woman becoming as one in Maurice Tabard's *The Walking Tree* (1947; p. 159). Living pillars of vegetation become the option of fashion photography in Michael Roberts's depiction of Manolo Blahnik's Leaf Shoes (1985; p. 163).

If it was only the fantasy of nature that was compelling to the Surrealists and not nature itself, the forest provided a perfect exemplar. Not only its sinister darkness and uncertainty could be suggested, but also its leafy fertility. The prelapsarian nudity that Delvaux associated with the tree could make of all dress the counterpart to the foliage—fig leaf leafage.

The woman as an expression of ideal beauty is associated as well with the flower. When feminine beauty is presented as the natural beauty of the flower, the woman becomes the radiant form of a Christian Lacroix Rose Hat (1986; p. 172), a Thierry Mugler Begonia Dress (1981–82; p. 170), or a Cristobal Balenciaga *Chou* cape (1967; p. 179), as if in natural reversion to beautiful form. While the swirling and fertile forms of nature have always been seen in relation to ideal female beauty, the concept was especially attractive to the Surrealist desire for analogues, understandings that might arise from dreams, representations of feminine beauty that are antirational, and the ever-present need to affiliate the natural with the beautiful. While many of the Surrealists were misogynists and clinically descriptive of women, nature nevertheless offered the sublime paradigm of woman in flower.

The butterfly was the Surrealist symbol of metamorphosis its transformation from the terrestrial to the transcendent paradoxically coupled with more sinister possibilities, as in Ernst's *And the Butterflies Begin to Sing* (1929; p. 180), where the *memento mori* signals the insect's demise. In fashion, the butterfly likewise assumed a life more symbolic than that of merely decorative usage or pattern, its erupting three-dimensionally from the surface of Schiaparelli garments giving testimony to its new role. The design brought the butterfly to almost every part of the body, including butterfly gloves, soaring butterflies on a hat, and an echelon of butterfly buttons on a suit jacket (p. 171). Their obstinate three-dimensionality gives them flight, but also the role of a semi-autonomous sculpture within the article of clothing. The light or alighting perch of the butterfly on the garment assures the sculptural integrity of the butterfly as an object, a form rather than just a design.

Among such transformations, one of the most plausible and elegant was the equation of woman and bird, the feathers of hat and/or dress, the lightness of flight, and even the presence of bird cages corroborating the possibilities of the bird as metaphor for the woman of beauty.

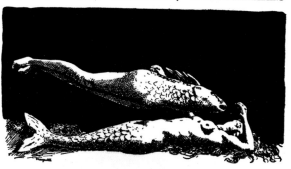

Announcement for Surrealist Exhibition, Brussels, 1945–46

Always a leading city for Surrealism and the home of René Magritte and Paul Delvaux, Brussels emerged from the Second World War with significant and tenacious proclivities for Surrealist art and literature. This exhibition announcement "embodies" the fish, which serves as partner to the mermaid, each a composite of figure and fish.

MAN RAY (American, 1890–1976)
Ball at the Château of the Vicomte de Noailles,
Grasse, 1929
Photograph
Man Ray Archives, Paris

A sea motif prevailed at this costume ball, held
at the Noailles villa during the filming of *Les
Mystères du Château du Dé*, by Man Ray. The
photographer reclines in front and the host
stands in the center back. Until the beginning
of the Second World War, legendary Surrealist
parties and fêtes, at which decorum was
abandoned, attracted the aristocratic,
powerful, and creative, and provided the
perfect setting for revolutionary styles of dress.

BELOW
DONATELLA (Italian)
Carp Dress, 1982
Photograph Roxanne Lowit

The designer poses in her own creation in the
compatible setting of a fish store in Hoboken,
New Jersey.

RENE MAGRITTE (Belgian, 1898–1967)
Song of Love, c. 1950–51
Oil on canvas, 30½ × 38⅝ in.
Museum of Contemporary Art, Chicago
Partial Gift of Joseph and Jory Shapiro

Magritte's love story, simultaneously human
and fish, suggests the origin of love to be an
inexplicable hybrid of the rational and
irrational.

GEORGE PLATT LYNES (American, 1907–1965)
Salvador Dali, c. 1939
Photograph

In a photographic fantasy, Dali combines living model with live lobsters. As fascinated by the lobster's atavistic grotesquery as by its association with genitalia, Dali hides behind the model in an image of passive aggression. In adopting the lobster as symbol, Dali took license with Surrealist concepts and sympathies and developed a personal iconography.

SALVADOR DALI (Spanish, born 1904)
Lobster Telephone, 1936
Mixed media, actual size
The Tate Gallery, London

ELSA SCHIAPARELLI
Organza Dress with Painted Lobster, 1937
Philadelphia Museum of Art
Photograph Taishi Hirokawa

Schiaparelli, with the assistance of Dali,
depicted the lobster with a certain demureness.
It does not come directly from sea but has
entered the world of edibles, having been
cooked to its rose-pink color and set in a field of
parsley. Its potentially sinister aspect is thus
mitigated, but not entirely absent, in the
traditional manner of Surrealist provocation,
which allows a party dress to conjure up icons.

146

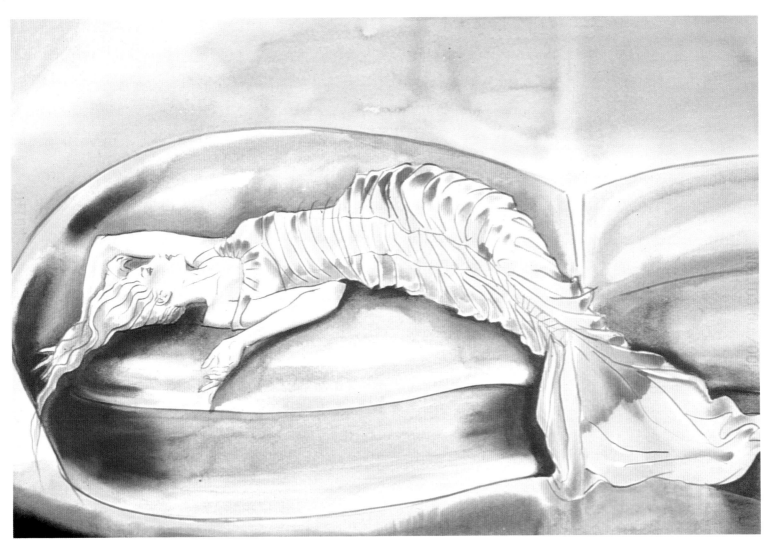

ABOVE
CHARLES JAMES (American, born
England, 1906–1978)
Siren-Crustacean Dress, on James's Butterfly
Sofa
Watercolor on paper by Antonio
Published *Vanity*, Milan, April 1982

Antonio's illustration of the dress by designer
James renders it as a segmented crustacean in its
languorous passage from the depths to a sofa
emulating Dali's famous lip design.
Furthermore, the dress is rose, in reference to
the cooked lobster of the Schiaparelli gown.

RIGHT
SALVADOR DALI
Study for Jewelry: Leaf-Veined Case, Unicorn
Brooch, Mobile, and Lobster Bracelet, 1949
Pencil and watercolor on paper
Minami Art Museum, Tokyo

In Dali's jewelry designs he indicates his
preoccupation with the forms of nature, seeing
the leaf as an analogue for the human hand,
synthesizing the natural and unnatural worlds
to make a unicorn brooch, and devising what
becomes the perfect accessory to the 1937
Schiaparelli dress in the lobster bracelet.

TOP LEFT
ADAM KURTZMAN (American, born 1957)
Fish Hat in Window Display, Barney's, New York, 1986

Shown in both boutiques and art galleries, Kurtzman's hats are both art and apparel.

BELOW RIGHT
CINZIA RUGGIERI (Italian, born 1953)
Dress with Octopus, 1984

Perhaps not even Dali in the 1930s would have been so perversely inventive with the creatures of the sea.

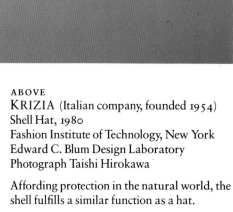

ABOVE
KRIZIA (Italian company, founded 1954)
Shell Hat, 1980
Fashion Institute of Technology, New York
Edward C. Blum Design Laboratory
Photograph Taishi Hirokawa

Affording protection in the natural world, the shell fulfills a similar function as a hat.

LEFT
ADAM KURTZMAN
Manta Hat, 1986
Photograph Noelle Hoeppe

ABOVE
YVES SAINT LAURENT (French, born
Algeria 1936)
Sardine Dress, 1983
Photograph Claus Ohm

Sequining in a fish-scale pattern creates a
shimmering, subtle suggestion of marine
marvels and beauty.

RIGHT
FRANÇOIS LESAGE (French, born 1929)
Sardine-Can Handbag and Fish Belt, 1987

As the embroidered imbrications of the garment
create sardines of Saint Laurent dresses, so the
Lesage embroidery creates not only the fishes
but their trompe l'oeil presentation in a can
with its lid being folded back.

CHRISTIAN LACROIX
Divine Folly (for Jean Patou), 1985
Photograph Roxanne Lowit

Acclaimed for his adventurous design at the
Parisian House of Patou (where Karl Lagerfeld
and Jean-Paul Gaultier had once been
designers), Lacroix launched his own couture
house in 1987. At Patou his inventive design
often had a Surrealist cast. Trained as an art
historian and originally intending to be a
museum curator, he was subsequently drawn to
fashion, where his artistic impulses led to
dresses such as this, embodying the spirit of the
forest.

RIGHT
SALVADOR DALI
Leaf-Veined Hand Pendants, 1949
Sculpted gold with cabochon rubies and a
single cabochon emerald
Minami Art Museum, Tokyo

Symbolist poet Charles Baudelaire called
nature a temple where living columns
occasionally permit "confused" words. The
recourse to nature as a spiritual home and the
ultimate confusion between comprehension and
the natural order were touchstones of Surrealist
thought and represent the affinity of Surrealist
arts and letters with Symbolism.

BELOW RIGHT
CINZIA RUGGIERI
Weeds Dress, 1983

Ruggieri's dress puts the wearer in the authentic
habiliment of the first woman.

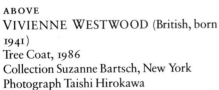

ABOVE
VIVIENNE WESTWOOD (British, born
1941)
Tree Coat, 1986
Collection Suzanne Bartsch, New York
Photograph Taishi Hirokawa

Beneath designer Westwood's tree coat there is
a tree dress with a face suggesting a tree spirit
within. The Surrealist imagination
encompassed the indwelling of spirits in nature.
For Westwood, the tree is more than pattern; it
is a process of conforming to nature and of
acknowledging animism in nature.

ADELLE LUTZ (American, born 1948)
Ivy Jacket with Wood Slacks, 1986
Published *Vanity Fair*, New York, October 1986
Photograph Annie Leibovitz

Lutz's camouflage, worn by David Byrne,
blatantly fails in its chameleon objective of
readapting and absorbing the figure into the
natural environment.

BRUCE WEBER (American, born 1946)
Dress by Karl Lagerfeld, 1984
Photograph

Twigs and moss become not surface decoration
but the setting for a dress by Karl Lagerfeld and
its embroidery by the hand of nature.

A. M. CASSANDRE (French, born the Ukraine, 1901–1968)
Cover for *Harper's Bazaar*, New York, July 1938

Graphic designer Cassandre merged the dressmaker's art with images from the sea in this *Harper's Bazaar* cover; a veil becomes a net and a mannequin becomes a hybrid of sea and dress form—a mer-form.

MIGUEL COVARRUBIAS (Mexican, born 1904)
Cover for *Vogue*, New York, July 1, 1937

A bather wearing a wool-jersey bathing suit by Sacony transcends the waters but also floats with a bather's grace.

EILEEN AGAR (British, born 1904)
Ceremonial Hat for Eating Bouillabaisse, c. 1938
Courtesy Birch and Conran Fine Art, London

Surrealist artist Agar inverted a cork basket to
create the structure of a hat compounded of
shells, coral, and other collage elements.

MAN RAY
Marie-Laure, Vicomtesse de Noailles, c. 1930
Photograph
Courtesy Robert Miller Gallery, New York

The Vicomtesse de Noailles, noted for her
adventuresome style of dress, wears a costume
in the form of a squid.

CHRISTIAN LACROIX (French, born
1951)
Sketch for Shell Hat (for Jean Patou), 1984–85
Ink on paper, with engraving

Stapled to Lacroix's drawing is an illustration
of a shell used as inspiration for his twisting
form.

CHANEL'S IMMACULATE SHELL OF WHITE
GROSGRAIN. JAY THORPE.

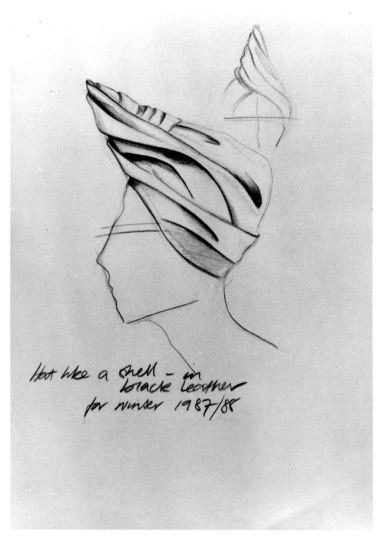

Hat like a shell — in
black leather
for winter 1987/88

MARCEL VERTES (French, born Hungary, 1895–1961)
White-Grosgrain Shell Hat, by Gabrielle (Coco) Chanel, 1938
Published *Harper's Bazaar*, New York, January 1938

Although Chanel (1883–1971) was a friend of many Surrealists and traveled in the circles connecting art and fashion in Paris for several decades, her fashions seldom assumed a Surrealist cast. A singular instance is the shell hat affiliating her with the seashell motif of the early Surrealists.

KIRSTEN WOODWARD (British, born 1960)
Sketch for Hat Like a Shell, in Black Leather, 1986–87
Ink on paper

British hat designer Woodward employs leather in a turban-style configuration that has the shell as its ultimate source. Woodward's hat designs often simulate coiffures (see p. 32) and recreate objects in leather and other millinery materials.

LEFT
DOROTHEA TANNING (American, born 1912)
The Birthday, 1942
Oil on canvas, 40⅛ × 25⅝ in.
Collection of the artist

Tanning, who met Max Ernst in 1942 and became his wife in 1946, presents a cryptic, mythic, and perhaps even autobiographic tree-woman, who has roots in nature but also lives in a world of mystery.

OPPOSITE
MAURICE TABARD (French, 1897–1984)
The Walking Tree, 1947
Photomontage
Courtesy Lucien Treillard, Paris

In Surrealist photographer Tabard's image, the reflection of a tree assumes the silhouette and structure of a dress—a play on words between tree trunk and body's trunk.

PAUL DELVAUX (Belgian, born 1897)
Birth of the Day, 1937
Oil on canvas, 47¼ × 59¼ in.
The Peggy Guggenheim Collection, Venice
Solomon R. Guggenheim Foundation, New
York

Perceiving woman as the personification of day,
Delvaux gives her roots and a woodgrain base
from which the torso grows. In this, his
archaism and passive obsession with women is
made manifest. Delvaux is able to show
complete nudity and yet conceal the genitals as
if they were dressed in the clothes of nature. It is
difficult to look upon these tree skirts as high
art in view of their roughly contemporary
counterparts in the animated trees of Walt
Disney, but Delvaux sees the living tree with an
almost medieval earnestness of purpose.

RENE MAGRITTE
Discovery, c. 1928
Oil on canvas, 25½ × 19¾ in.
Private collection, Brussels

The revelation of this painting, which Magritte
pronounces a discovery and not the more
customary Surrealist ambiguity, seems to be the
affinity between woman and nature. In making
her alternatively woodgrain and physical form,
Magritte plays with the conventions of Cubist
collage established some two decades earlier
but asserts the primacy of the figure and the
spiritual connection between figure and natural
world.

MAX ERNST
Caresse Crosby, 1932
Gouache and pencil on wood, 9 × 7½ in.
Collection Mr. and Mrs. Marshall Padorr,
Chicago

Ernst permits the perceptual play between the
natural grain of the wood and the supposition
that such grain may only be surface pattern—
leaving room for the ever-present uncertainty
about the truth of the object and its fictions.
Caresse Crosby and her husband Harry were
the owners of Black Sun Press, which published
many Surrealist books in America.

max ernst

PAUL DELVAUX (Belgian, born 1897)
Call of the Night, 1938
Oil on canvas, 43¼ × 57⅛ in.
Collection Anthony Penrose, Chiddingly,
England

As the day yields to night in Delvaux's parable
of time's passage, the treetop branches affix
themselves to the figures' heads and the trees
stand denuded in the background.

MAN RAY (American, 1890–1976)
Rien dans le puis du Nord, 1935
Photograph
Man Ray Archives, Paris

Whereas the subconscious offered the ideal
reintegration of man with his natural
emotional and intellectual state, the new
assimilation of nature could assume form as
figures become a part of nature.

MANOLO BLAHNIK (Spanish, born 1943)
Leaf Shoes, 1985
Published *Tatler*, London, December 1985–
January 1986
Photograph Michael Roberts

The comfort, quiet, and stealth of natural
walking are evoked in Blahnik's leaf shoes,
made of the softest natural materials. In this
photograph the shoes, partially camouflaged by
the bark, hang from the tree as if natural
protuberances—or tree caterpillars in slow
descent. Similarly, model Jason Connery is
laced into nature by his idealized lattice of ivy.

GENE MOORE (American, born 1910)
Window Display, Kenneth Beauty Salon,
New York, 1970
Photograph Malan Studio, Inc.

Display artist Moore created a fantastic bird's
nest as hair for the hair salon of Kenneth.

BRUCE WEBER
Dress by Karl Lagerfeld, 1984
Photograph

To the assumption that fashion is artifice,
Weber provides the axiom that clothing finds
itself in complete harmony with nature.
Distinguished as a naturalist photographer,
Weber plays here with the synthesis of the
natural and antinatural.

INTERNATIONAL SURREALIST BULLETIN
No. 4 ISSUED BY THE SURREALIST GROUP IN ENGLAND
PUBLIE PAR LE GROUPE SURREALISTE EN ANGLETERRE
BULLETIN INTERNATIONAL DU SURREALISME
PRICE ONE SHILLING   SEPTEMBER 1936

THE INTERNATIONAL SURREALIST EXHIBITION

L'EXPOSITION INTERNATIONAL DU SURRÉALISME

TOP
Title Page from *International Surrealist Bulletin*, London, No. 4, September 1936
Courtesy Zabriskie Gallery, New York

Celebrating the exhibition at the New Burlington Galleries, London, of June 11–July 4, 1936, the *International Surrealist Bulletin* places a flowering head in the midst of Trafalgar Square.

BOTTOM
PAUL DELVAUX
Pygmalion, 1939
Oil on canvas
Musée d'Art Moderne, Brussels

OPPOSITE
PAUL DYSON (British, born 1951)
Window Display, Harvey Nichols, London
Photograph Anthony Lawrence

Conceived in emulation of Dali, the window designed by Paul Dyson in association with Mark Langston demonstrates the continuity of Surrealist themes in British design, acknowledging Surrealist appropriation as a matter for easy recognition by the viewer.

ABOVE
SALVADOR DALI
Cover of *Vogue*, New York, June 1, 1939

The floriate head of the 1936 *International Surrealist Bulletin* reappears on the cover of *Vogue* three years later.

BELOW AND OPPOSITE
JOHN GALLIANO (British, born 1962)
Clock Wig, 1985
Magpie-Nest Wig, 1985
Photograph Martin Brading

In two extravagant hairpieces (below and opposite), Galliano, working in collaboration with Amanda Grieve, finds the counterpart to his highly intelligent clothing filled with wit and with knowledge of the history of art and of clothing.

TOP AND CENTER
DANUTA RYDER (Polish, born 1952)
Window Display, Henri Bendel, New York, 1986

Not scarecrows but wood spirits seem to exist in a Manhattan store window.

THIERRY MUGLER (French, born 1948)
Flora (Begonia), 1981–82
Photograph Roxanne Lowit

The dress and the wearer become the flower, a
soft transformation of the entire figure.

ELSA SCHIAPARELLI (French, born Italy,
1890–1973)
Bug Necklace, c. 1937–38
The Brooklyn Museum, New York
Photograph Irving Solero

The transparency of the necklace would allow
one to think that the bugs are crawling directly
on the neck, in a macabre concept of fashion.
Although Schiaparelli may have drawn
inspiration from scarab jewelry in Egyptian art,
her interpretation of the theme is markedly
cryptic and discomforting.

THIERRY MUGLER
Flora (Bouquet), 1981–82
Photograph Roxanne Lowit

Of a fantasy exceeding even that of Walter
Crane, Flora becomes the complete dress of the
figure, and the wearer is either the flower or the
spirit-dweller therein.

TOP RIGHT
ELSA SCHIAPARELLI
Jacket with Cicada Buttons, Autumn 1938
The Metropolitan Museum of Art, New York
The Costume Institute
Photograph Taishi Hirokawa

Schiaparelli's modern scarabs function as fastenings.

RIGHT
ELSA SCHIAPARELLI
Jacket with Butterfly Buttons, 1937
Photograph Hideoki

A formation of butterflies takes wing on a Schiaparelli jacket. A tireless investigator of the world of nature, Schiaparelli seldom translated nature into decorative pattern, but rather saw it as incarnate on the garment.

OPPOSITE
ISSEY MIYAKE (Japanese, born 1938)
Butterfly Dress, 1982

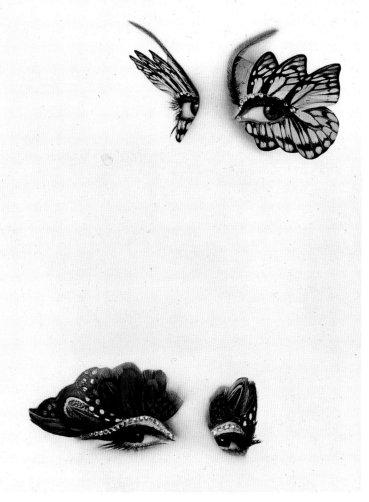

ABOVE LEFT
CHRISTIAN LACROIX
Rose Hat (for Jean Patou), 1986
Photograph Oliviero Toscani

A brilliant explosion of petals subsumes the figure in Lacroix's hat.

ABOVE RIGHT
BERT STERN (American, born 1929)
Butterfly Eyes, 1964
Photograph
Published *Vogue*, New York, December 15, 1964

CHRISTOPHE TONY THORIMBERT
(Swiss, born 1957)
Fashion Editorial, 1986
Published *Uomo Harper's Bazaar*, Milan,
November–December 1986

The perversity of the seductress with turkey
head gives an edge to the presentation of men's
clothing that the subject itself often lacks.

BERT STERN
Fashion Photograph, 1965
Published *Vogue*, New York, January 1, 1965

Stern attributes sovereign plumage to the
woman of animal grace and of natural beauty.

YVES SAINT LAURENT (French, born Algeria 1936)
"Bouquet" Bridal Gown in White Gazar, 1980

Traditional associations with the bride as embodiment of spring are amplified by Saint Laurent's elegant transformation of the bride into the full presence of nature in flower.

Cover of *Flair*, New York, May 1950

The die-cut covers of *Flair* customarily opened to reveal something quite different on the inside. Thus, the outer petals of the flower become the woman at their center.

FLAIR

MAY 1950

THE MONTHLY MAGAZINE
FIFTY CENTS

Advertisement for Calugi e Giannelli
Published *Vanity*, Milan, November–December
1986

Nature, having always provided the literal
means for reflection, affords as well the
opportunity to oscillate between the image of
woman and flower.

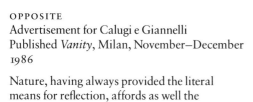

RIGHT
CRISTOBAL BALENCIAGA (French, born
Spain, 1895–1972)
Black Gazar *Chou* Cape, 1967
Photograph Kublin
Courtesy Archives Balenciaga, Paris

An efflorescent garment atop the long narrow
stem of the body simulates a most exotic garden
flower.

MAX ERNST
And the Butterflies Begin to Sing, plate 120
from *La Femme 100 Têtes*, 1929
Collage-novel, published Paris, 1929

The metamorphosis of caterpillar to butterfly—
the transformation of the commonplace into the
beautiful—is mitigated by the tandem
representation of the sinister and perverse. The
title of Ernst's book is typical of his puns: it
may be read as "The Hundred-Headed
Woman" or "The Woman without (*sans*) a
Head."

GENE MOORE (American, born 1910)
Butterflies and Egg, Window Display,
Tiffany & Co., New York, 1980

Peggy Guggenheim, Venice, 1968
Photograph David Seymour
Published *Vanity Fair*, New York, February
1986

Wearing fanciful butterfly sunglasses, Peggy
Guggenheim, friend and patron of Surrealist
artists, posed on the roof of her palazzo on the
Grand Canal, Venice. Her New York gallery,
Art of This Century, provided an important
venue for Surrealist artists between 1942 and
1947.

SALVADOR DALI

Fashion Advertisement, 1946
Published *Vogue*, New York, July 1946

The butterfly motif was favored by the
Surrealists, in particular by Dali, whose zeal for
the creature's flamboyant beauty took
precedence here over connations of the
transformed and ugly.

B STANDS FOR BEAUTY...BE IT BUTTERFLIES OR BEAUTIFUL *Bryans* BEAUTIFUL THE *BREATHTAKING* NYLONS!

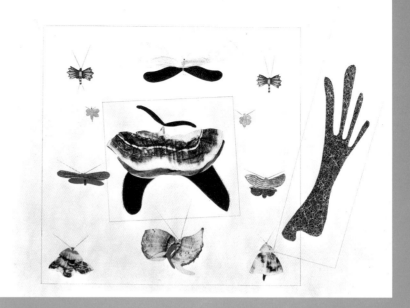

MAX ERNST
Butterflies, 1931 or 1933
Collage, oil, gouache, and pencil on paper,
19¾ × 25¾ in.
The Museum of Modern Art, New York
Purchase

SALVADOR DALI
Fashion Advertisement, 1957
Published *Harper's Bazaar*, October 1957

The butterfly transformed in Surrealist collage
and advertising.

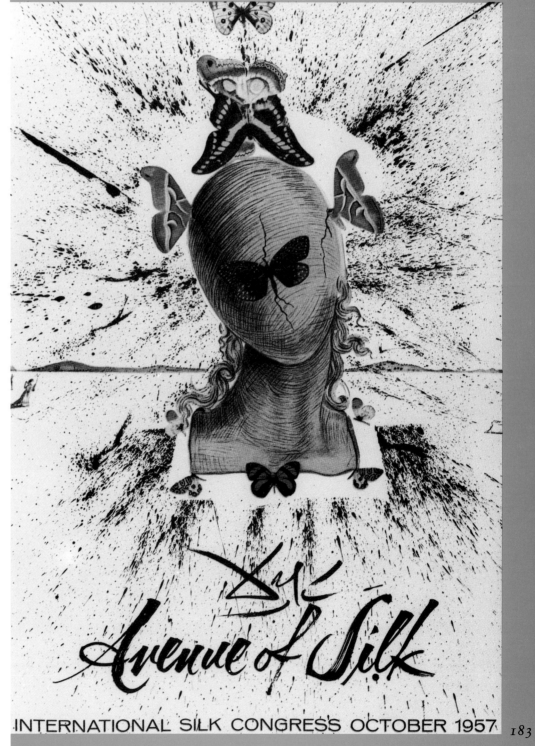

INTERNATIONAL SILK CONGRESS OCTOBER 1957

JEAN-CHARLES DE CASTELBAJAC
(French, born Morocco 1950)
Eagle Dress, 1986

The plumage of the bird is the source of the
metaphor, but the imagery is operative even in
the form of the bird itself.

MAN RAY
Elsa Schiaparelli, c. 1934
Photograph
Man Ray Archives, Paris

Although Schiaparelli was associated with
some of the maddest adventures in Surrealist
dress, she also possessed serene grace, as in this
portrait by Man Ray. The birdlike character of
the portrait does not vitiate its dignity but
rather corroborates it.

GEORGE STAVRINOS (American, born 1948)
Advertisement for Bergdorf Goodman, New York, 1980
Graphite on paper

The wings of birds and Nike take flight amid broken columns in this contemporary fashion presentation.

February 1950

THE MONTHLY MAGAZINE   FIFTY CENTS

ABOVE AND OPPOSITE
Cover of *Flair*, New York, February 1950

The die-cut wing without provides a glimpse of the bird woman within.

ABOVE
ANTONIO
Design by Roberto Capucci, 1983
Published *Vanity*, Milan, April 1983

In the feathery touch of the gifted illustrator's
line, the woman becomes a bird.

OPPOSITE
THIERRY MUGLER
Feather Dresses, 1982
Photograph Scott Heiser

ABOVE
THIERRY MUGLER
Bird Dresses with Bird Cage, 1982
Photograph Niall McInerney

OPPOSITE
MAX ERNST
The Robing of the Bride, 1940
Oil on canvas, 51 × 37⅞ in.
The Peggy Guggenheim Collection, Venice
Solomon R. Guggenheim Foundation,
New York
Photograph Carmalo Guadagno

In Ernst's conception, the vestment of the bride
is her metamorphosis into a bird.

LEFT

LEFT
RENE MAGRITTE
The Therapeutist, 1937
Oil on canvas, 35½ × 25½
Urvator Collection, Belgium

The substitution of bird cage for figure offers a Surrealist adventure in interpretation. In assigning a particular psychoanalytic association to the image (yet avoiding a specific interpretation), Magritte affords himself the luxury of therapy through symbol, even in the enigma of an itinerant figure who imprisons birds.

OPPOSITE ABOVE
ENGLISH ECCENTRICS (British, founded 1984)
Fashion Presentation, 1986

A canny group of young British designers calling themselves the English Eccentrics self-consciously keep the spirit of Surrealism alive, not only in their design but also in the manner of their runway presentations. They plumb Dada and Surrealist sources for an avowedly eccentric style.

OPPOSITE BELOW
ANDRE MASSON (French, born 1896)
Mannequin with Bird Cage, 1938
Photograph Man Ray
Man Ray Archives, Paris

Among the mannequins created for the 1938 *Exposition Internationale du Surréalisme* in Paris, Masson's is one of the most cryptic in its contrasts of liberty and caging.

JEAN-CHARLES DE CASTELBAJAC
Seagull Coat Worn by Dianne B., Winter
1980—81
Photograph Robert Mapplethorpe

Castelbajac sets his seagulls free with abandon
as the uppermost gull emerges three-
dimensionally from the coat as if to soar beyond
the garment, an ultimate testimony to the flight
of a Surrealist ambition to be in clothing and to
surpass it.

MARCEL ROCHAS (French, 1902–1955)
Bird Dress, 1934
Photograph Harry Meerson
Published *Harper's Bazaar*, New York, April 1934

A bird, Charles Lamb wrote, "appears a
thoughtless thing," and Rochas's bird seems to
have been set free with an elegance and grace of
flight to accentuate the airy/aery lightness of the
wearer.

DOYENNE
AND DANDY

For Elsa Schiaparelli, it was more passion than fashion. The energy, "moment," and inspiration of her work were more important than a line or the development of a style. Her clothing is an expression of desire, not merely of design. Although Schiaparelli maintained her own business over a quarter of a century, she is preeminently remembered for a first trompe l'oeil gesture of 1928—a sweater—and for her bravura work of the late 1930s. What lies between these breathtakingly bold, brilliant achievements are lesser efforts and a terrain of intriguing yet uninspired clothes. But when Schiaparelli was good, she was sensational.

In some measure, Schiaparelli acknowledged the momentary and inspired nature of her creation when she discussed design in her autobiography *Shocking Life*:

Dress designing . . . is to me not a profession but an art. I found it was a most difficult and unsatisfying art, because as soon as the dress is born it has already become a thing of the past. . . . A dress has no life of its own unless it is worn, and as soon as this happens another personality takes over from you and animates it, or tries to, glorifies it or destroys it, or makes it into a song of beauty. More often it becomes an indifferent object, or even a pitiful caricature of what you wanted it to be—a dream, an expression.

Conversant with mysticism as much as with the atelier, Schiaparelli ascribed near-magical inspiration to the creation of clothing. Born in Rome of aristocratic parents in 1890, she knew the world of the spirit and perceived the post-sacred era largely in terms of mystical cause and magical effects. In 1914 she married William de Wendt de Kerlor, a theosophist; smitten and "spellbound," she had heard him lecture in London on "the powers of the soul over the body, of magic and eternal youth." *Shocking Life* is told as if she were in an out-of-body trance, observing her lifetime at a spiritualized remove and presenting her story with moralizing (and memorializing) tales. In accounts of her work, there is a suggestion of recurring exhilarations and enthusiasms about new ideas in design, but not of an evolving concept for her clothes. By this disposition and by its design consequences, she was ever the artistic designer, seizing at ideas, grasping many with a quickness of gesture; but she was not the refined designer, cogitating and coaxing a style from a garment. Instead, verve, vivacity, and the supreme instantaneous moment operated for Schiaparelli— always an elation, never a dilation. Her self-conscious equation

OPPOSITE
HORST P. HORST (American, born Germany 1906)
Elsa Schiaparelli, 1937
Photograph

Schiaparelli, preeminent figure in Surrealist fashion design, posed in Horst's ambiguous mirror–picture frame.

of the designer's objective with that of the artist is at the heart of her work. She believed that the garment was the place for artistic expression rather than the medium for the couturier's craft. To be sure, she employed some of the world's finest craftspersons—such as the splendid embroiderers of the House of Lesage—but she herself was never a craftswoman.

What is important about Schiaparelli is that she dared and dreamed, allowing clothing created out of pure, unmitigated, almost divine inspiration to become a choice for twentieth-century dress. Her influence today is widely felt in the witty, imaginative work of Karl Lagerfeld, the fabulous *folies* of Christian Lacroix, and the chicly clever masterpieces of Yves Saint Laurent.

Schiaparelli's inspired moments had a tinge of perversity. Her festive 1938 collections, the Pagan, Harlequin, and especially the Circus collection, seem to the fashion historian a testament to the perverse. As Europe headed toward war, Schiaparelli went to the circus, an adventure filled with beauty but also with naughty insouciance to the sober world outside a circus tent. The Circus collection—prime examples from it were shown in the exhibition *Moments de Mode* (1986), which inaugurated the Musée des Arts de la Mode in Paris—included fitted jackets, a backward suit (p. 208), a suit appliquéd with diagonal stripes of fur, "tent" veils, prints of balloons and clowns, and embroidered boleros with sequences of acrobats, posing elephants, and prancing horses. Summer 1938 would seem a strange season for such frolic, but Schiaparelli's inspiration knew no season nor world-clock. She was at her most inspired in that year, owing to her association, perhaps, with many artists, decorators, and illustrators, including Christian Bérard, Jean-Michel Frank, Salvador Dali, Jean Cocteau (pp. 202, 204, 205), and Etienne de Beaumont. Such relationships were clearly stimulating to Schiaparelli, but they were equally important for the artists themselves. Etienne de Beaumont worked with Schiaparelli on jewelry in 1938; when he later designed the costumes for the *Circus Polka* (1942), George Balanchine's choreography for the performing elephants of the Ringling Brothers Circus in New York's Madison Square Garden, he must have realized how farsighted Schiaparelli's inventions in 1938 had been. At her most irrepressible at a time when Nazi rallies were supplanting circuses, Schiaparelli fulfilled a destiny without time. For her as for many great visual artists and writers, anything even glimpsed as possible became an aesthetic necessity; the idea must be seized, and it must be realized as soon as it is perceived. Picasso, reviewing his early Cubist work, remarked in 1923: "To search means nothing in painting. To find is the thing." This avowal of artistic discovery could also describe Schiaparelli's special genius.

Schiaparelli's first design combined inspiration and improvisation with little likelihood of realization, despite her headstrong determination to do what she thought she might do. It was a trompe l'oeil sweater created from a quick sketch; a black-wool model, it had a simulation of a white butterfly bow at the neck. Schiaparelli was apparently as startled as anyone else by the immediate success of the sweater and had no resource at hand for producing the popular garment herself. She recruited a group of Armenian women to knit according to her design. On receiving demands for a knitted skirt to go along with it, Schiaparelli reportedly accepted orders for a product she could not conceive of making and recruited many more

ELSA SCHIAPARELLI
Snuff Flacon, c. 1939
Collection Tina Chow, New York
Photograph Taishi Hirokawa

Schiaparelli's fragrance for men, called Snuff, came in tobacco-brown packaging, and the flacon—this, after all, is not a pipe—was surrounded by brown tissue, perhaps to reassure hesitant masculine customers.

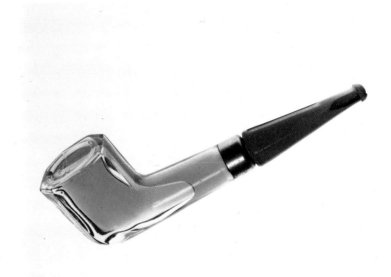

RENE MAGRITTE (Belgian, 1898–1967)
The Betrayal of Images, 1929
Oil on canvas, 23¼ × 31½ in.
Los Angeles County Museum of Art

Although Schiaparelli made the strange new concept of male cologne more familiar by her pipe, Magritte's odd inscription, "Ceci n'est pas une pipe" (This is not a pipe), suddenly makes the familiar strange.

Armenian women, filling orders in a frenzy. For the skirts, she claims to have bought "good and cheap material in the bargain counter" at the Galeries Lafayette in Paris. In an industry of legends, this tale is especially noteworthy. A novice without design experience, not even able to secure materials at wholesale, Schiaparelli was immediately catapulted to fashion attention. With the promotion of the writer Anita Loos and others, the trompe l'oeil sweater became an international hit. In her description of the sweater, the designer feigned indifference to its meaning: "It was the time when abstract Dadaism and Futurism were the talk of the world, the time when chairs looked like tables, and tables like footstools, when it was not done to ask what a painting represented or what a poem meant." But this account is somewhat ingenuous, for although Schiaparelli was not yet part of the circle of artists and writers in Paris, she was aware of the powerful forces of vanguard art at the time. Her willful illusionism was not without precedent for fashion, and in 1928 it succeeded as a perfect gesture of art, artifice, and apparel. Variations on the idea followed, and illusionism lurked behind many of Schiaparelli's designs. Nevertheless the trompe l'oeil sweater was a one-time thrill, an invention, a fad. We all know, said Corneille, how the French love novelty. Schiap's sweater was as much a novelty as Duchamp's bottlerack, a readymade lesson in art, a specific moment in history.

The business Schiaparelli founded on the rue de la Paix in Paris flourished in sportswear, tailored clothing, and evening wear. The early 1930s represented a consolidation of techniques for Schiaparelli, as she increasingly brought together expert craftsmen for the couture. The coalescence of a skilled atelier meant a finished garment and excellent construction following from Schiaparelli's talents as an inventor. The designer kept some edge to the creation by her particular interest in unusual materials. She was indefatigable in finding new fabrics for fashion, especially manmade fibers that announced their difference from the accustomed natural stuffs. She chose a cellophanelike fabric simulating glass, which played with illusions of transparency and the hard rendered soft and defied all conventional notions about the properties of material. The House of Colcombet in Lyons created to Schiaparelli's specifications a newspaper-clipping fabric (printed with news stories about the designer) setting up a friction between the expectation of paper and ink and the reality of the softness of fabric. These inventions were complemented by a range of accessories made in accordance with Schiaparelli's whims and incredible inventions. Lucite illusions in costume jewelry and buttons; hand bags as bird cages (in 1936); ceramic vegetables and even aspirins as necklaces (the latter designed in collaboration with Surrealist poet Louis Aragon) were in Schiaparelli's vast repertory of accessories, many of which had more to do with making a statement than with being worn on city streets. Nonetheless, throughout the 1930s Schiaparelli gathered an affluent, adventurous clientele that bought with a recklessness almost as free as the designer's imagination. In that decade Paris was the site of the great Surrealist balls, which, in their mixture of masquerade with couture elegance, provided the perfect context for Schiaparelli's innovations and illusions. If fancy-dress Surrealism was not enough to stimulate Schiaparelli's imagination, the Surrealism of life in 1930s Paris would have affirmed her ambition to let the synthetic stand for the natural and the bizarre take the place of the expected.

Furthermore, Schiaparelli was as ready to accept the real as

OPPOSITE
KARL LAGERFELD (French, born Germany 1938)
Candelabrum Dress, 1985
Photograph Michael Roberts
Published *Tatler*, London, December–January 1986

As the symbol and guide for a perfume named Sleeping may be a single candlestick, so an evening dress may require the full-scale illumination of a candelabrum. Lagerfeld's romantic evocation is, like Schiaparelli's, anachronistic.

MARCEL VERTES (French, born Hungary, 1895–1961)
Advertisement for Sleeping, by Elsa Schiaparelli, c. 1940
Published *Harper's Bazaar*, New York, March 15, 1940

The candle, renamed *le plafond* (the ceiling) in Magritte's *Dreaming's Key* (p. 106), "lights the way to ecstasy," according to Schiaparelli's advertising copy. The literalism of the candle shape is reinforced by the packaging in the form of a candle snuff. The candle not only suggests nocturnal reverie but also the transition between the darkly subconscious and the illumined conscious.

Schiaparelli a fait cette robe pour la danse, je l'ai copiée pour le Harper's Bazaar. Jean ☆

1937

PARIS

Schiaparelli might have cut this tapering sheath for Madame Tallien. A slit for the wrist, a brilliant new color... cyclamen.

OPPOSITE
JEAN COCTEAU (French, 1889–1963)
Dress by Elsa Schiaparelli, 1937
Published *Harper's Bazaar*, New York,
September 15, 1937

Art and fashion intersected as Cocteau designed
for Schiaparelli and also illustrated her work for
Harper's Bazaar. Cocteau identified his role in
this drawing with a precision Magritte would
have admired: "Schiaparelli made this dress for
the dance and I copied it for *Harper's Bazaar*."

ABOVE RIGHT
ELSA SCHIAPARELLI (French, born Italy,
1890–1973)
Fragrance Flacons, 1937–48
Collection Tina Chow, New York
Photograph Taishi Hirokawa

Schiaparelli evoked Surrealist notions regarding
fragrance, dream, and language in her bottles
for the perfumes Shocking (1937), Sleeping
(1938), and Zut (1948). The Shocking and Zut
flacons take their shapes from the body, so that
by inversion fragrance emanates from within
rather than from the surface of the body. The
bottle for Sleeping takes the form of a candle, an
allusion to the world of dream. Language plays
a role, as well: the names of all the perfumes
begin with a sibillant sound, and all but Zut, an
expletive, were exotically titled in English, even
for the French market.

BELOW RIGHT
SALVADOR DALI
Fashion Advertisement for Bergdorf Goodman,
New York, 1943
Published *Vogue*, New York, October 1, 1943

Although it is really the scarf and other
accessories that are for sale, Surrealism offered
war-torn America and Europe dreams for sale
at a better price than any other illusion.

LEFT
SALVADOR DALI
Face-Chalice Profiles Pin, 1949
Gold
Minami Art Museûm, Tokyo

What could be embroidered on a coat could
also be fashioned in gold. Dali's image is the
same as that on the Cocteau-Schiaparelli coat.

ABOVE
ELSA SCHIAPARELLI
JEAN COCTEAU
Embroidered Evening Coat, c. 1937
Philadelphia Museum of Art
Photograph Taishi Hirokawa

In this collaboration between the designer and
the multifaceted artist, the cleverly embroidered
profiles of faces drawn by Cocteau form the
illusion of a vase. The embroidery was executed
by the House of Lesage, Paris.

Jean Cocteau decorates the back of Schiaparelli's coat

CECIL BEATON (British, 1904–1980)
Jean Cocteau–Elsa Schiaparelli Evening Coat,
1937
Published *Vogue*, New York, July 15, 1937

The complex network of artists surrounding
Schiaparelli included Beaton, whose illustration
of the evening coat on which Cocteau and
Schiaparelli collaborated was published in 1937.

she was to embrace the artificial. Her zealous use of the zipper, newly invented in 1936, was efficient and technological, but at the same time wondrously imaginative and innovative, as she incorporated the fastening into her design of a garment. Her artist *confrères* would readily play with the same idea, salaciously unzipping figures to see the naked body beneath, as if by aperture into flesh. A simple wool dress with a zipper in a contrasting color may not have been Surrealism at its most sublime, but it was novelty at its newest and invention at its most impudent. Schiaparelli's inventive promptings neither began nor ended with clothes and accessories. In 1934, she opened a London shop on Upper Grosvenor Street, where her displays were famous for their Surrealist tricks. Her Paris quarters on the Place Vendôme, which opened in 1936, became the place for Dali's shocking-pink bear (with drawers in the torso) perched on his Mae West Lip Sofa (p. 86). According to historian Caroline Milbank in *Couture*, the Paris shop's "window displays were likewise outré, something to see on the way to and from the Hotel Ritz, which was nearby." Today the Schiaparelli boutique, still in close proximity to the Ritz, seems tame in comparison to the hotel's own guests, who would outshine anything Schiaparelli could have dreamed of; but Paris in the 1930s was quite different. Schiaparelli's international reputation for high-style hi-jinks contrasted with the more understated clientele of the Ritz. Mrs. Reginald (Daisy) Fellowes, Millicent Rogers, and Lady Elsie Mendl were among her clients. She dressed movie stars both on- and off-screen.

Schiaparelli's great fashion frenzy with Mae West has become as legendary as the star herself, but the designer's account of the episode in her autobiography is uncharacteristically austere, offering this diffident and clinical description: "Mae West came to Paris. She was stretched out on the operating table of my workroom, and measured and probed with care and curiosity." The moment, in 1937, had its intensity, given Mae West's popularity in America and Europe at the time and given Schiaparelli's inventive desires regarding the hourglass silhouette—but also because of that encounter on a dissecting table. The Surrealist artist Leonor Fini created an hourglass-shaped bottle, based on the Mae West silhouette, for the new fragrance Schiaparelli dubbed "Shocking" in her predilection for names starting with "S" and her sensitivity to the effect of her work on some people. While Schiaparelli had been involved with licensing as early as 1934, perfume became an important foundation of her business thereafter (pp. 198, 200, 203). But her "shocking" clothing seldom offended in the 1930s. As Schiaparelli herself wrote of the 1938 collections in their independent, artistic themes: "The typical tempo of the time was marked by great enthusiasm. There was no criticism of 'Who can wear it?' As an amazing fact, Schiap did not lose a single one of her wealthy conservative old-fashioned clients but got a lot of new ones."

Although Schiaparelli had been shocking her clients for nearly a decade, the 1937–38 season was her moment to startle the world. She returned to trompe l'oeil with an invention so complete the body seemed to be embraced by another; her 1937 Jean Cocteau jacket (p. 100) incorporated head and hair that seemed to lean across the body of the wearer. With the inspiration of Dali, Schiaparelli created the remarkable lobster dress of 1937 (p. 146), a splendid giant lobster in an organdy field with parsley sprigs. Dali's lobster fully involved Schiaparelli in the Surrealist vocabulary of forms, offering the crustacean as aesthetic and animal surrogate of female sexuality. Schiaparelli offered the most discreet form of Dali's pixilated musings about the lobster and the woman and one of the most elegant servings of seafood ever made in dress form. Dali also designed the textile for Schiaparelli's tear dress (pp. 136–37) with the illusion of its having been torn repeatedly. For the master of slit eyeball, soft clock, and stained underwear, a tattered and torn dress seemed only mildly radical, but for the couture it was an insane and wild premise. Since then perhaps only Rei Kawakubo (p. 136) has matched the gesture in sheer and tearing eccentricity and audacity. In fact, it was Schiaparelli's 1937–38 association with artists that gave her special boldness, as if ideas were being generated by the artists and Schiaparelli became the natural creator of dresses in collaboration with their ideas. Butterflies flew into Schiaparelli's already vast zoo with artistic abandon because of her association with Surrealist artists, for whom the butterfly was the symbol of feminine beauty and of Surrealism's promised metamorphosis between beast and beauty.

With Dali, Schiaparelli invented both the Shoe Hat (p. 111) and the Mutton Chop Hat (p. 108). The Shoe Hat's topsy-turvy dislocation of purpose was and still is a great joke, but its elegance abides as well. Dali had been obsessed with shoes and their dislocation for a long time, but it was Schiaparelli who guided him to his supreme statement of the footloose pump. The hat was a personal favorite for Schiaparelli, who had Gala Dali photographed wearing it with a lips-embroidered suit, a perfect Surrealist ensemble. The Mutton Chop Hat, along with its cutlet-embroidered suit, was another of Dali's Surrealist suppers and allowed the couture to examine what its associations and its allusions might be. Schiaparelli's gesture was quietly subversive and outrageously creative. By the time of the three great fantasy collections of 1938, Schiaparelli was making clothing as an armature for ideas. Art seemed to be her preeminent thought. Her excellent workshops made severe structures of clothing, but the pink-and-blue children's world of the Circus collection, the lush naturalism and country and insect life of the Pagan collection, and the frolic (which became the name of Schiaparelli's purple lipstick) of the Harlequin collection created a last Parisian masquerade. Ideas cascaded over forms in the 1938 collections, both in clothing and accessories: in the Harlequin collection, a domino form became a hat and pockets became little nest-caches; in the Circus collection, the old Surrealist joke *attention à la peinture* (beware of fresh paint) is written on a dress; a hen nests coolly on a head (p. 113); and a hat becomes a quill pen and an inkwell (p. 109).

There can be no doubt that the 1937–38 season, at the juncture of art and war, was Schiaparelli's moment. On the reopening of the Paris salon after the Second World War, she offered examples of artistic clothing, but never with the inspired madness and exuberance of this brief efflorescence. A designer who was primarily a dressmaker would never have followed such an erratic pattern of achievement. No stylist would ignite such a flame, however briefly. Schiaparelli was

ABOVE
CECIL BEATON
Salvador and Gala Dali, 1937
Photograph
Courtesy Sotheby's, London

Beaton made a series of portraits in which he posed Dali and his wife Gala behind the artist's marionettelike landscape silhouettes.

OPPOSITE
SALVADOR DALI (Spanish, born 1904)
Cover for *Vogue*, New York, December 1, 1946

Art's illusions were commonplace in fashion periodicals of the 1940s, not only in clothing but also in graphics. Dali created faces within architecture in this holiday cover for *Vogue*, bringing the Surrealist vocabulary to vernacular forms.

different. She was distinctively an artist in the world of couture. She believed in inspiration and in the merger and magic of the arts together as a source of artistic germination. She managed artisans and dressmakers in her atelier, but she was not such a person herself. She was not a designer involved in the evolution of designs. She was an artist in the mystical tradition of creative inspiration and its consequence in art. A visionary, she touched clothing with the capacity to be art. Neither dressmaker nor designer, Schiaparelli gave clothing the romantic and inventive emancipation to become art even more than apparel.

As Meret Oppenheim had once offered as a Dada-Surrealist object her *Fur-Lined Tea Cup* (1936), so Salvador Dali offered his *Aphrodisiac Dinner Jacket* (1936), as much an object of consuming Surrealism as an invention of clothing. The dinner jacket with liquor glasses affixed to the surface is the counterpart to his creation with Schiaparelli of the Tear Dress and Fabric. In both, Dali brings the design and the object to the surface of the garment as if to determine what is internal and what external. As Schiaparelli was the doyenne of Surrealist fashion designers, Dali was her male counterpart. He collaborated with Schiaparelli in a succession of efforts in which it is difficult to determine the exact origin of the idea. In general, though, the inventions seem to be Dali's, as they come so resonantly from his body of work and from related avenues in Surrealism. The connections were manifold, and the artist's wife Gala was customarily dressed gratis by Schiaparelli, as she provided a perfect absurdist and plausible model for the designer's clothing.

Aside from Dali's specific creations of clothing, however, his idiosyncratic version of Surrealism was critical to the transmission of Surrealist concepts and themes into fashion. He was a dandy. Associating himself with the history of dandies, he fashioned his own appearance and assumed privilege, taking pleasure in inventing style for himself and for others. Dali's role in fashion was not only sanctioned by the Surrealist obsession with everyday life, but also with his responsibility to lead in style as the dandy-artist. Gala's role in fashion was largely derived from this same image—of the artist as arbiter of style in all matters.

The official Surrealists disavowed Dali, but their reasons for doing so did not touch upon his role in fashion. Nevertheless that role was intimately tied to his projection of an artistic temperament and to the part he played as an arbiter of style. It was, after all, Dali more than any official leader of Surrealism who opened up avenues to the fashion publications—requisite thoroughfares for Dali as a boulevardier. Breton, avatar of Surrealist intellect, had scant interest in Dali, avatar of Surrealist style. In fact, Breton repeatedly sought to disavow Dali's self-proclamation as a Surrealist. Dali's excesses (chiefly in the postwar period) in extravagance and commercialism do not vitiate the reasonableness of his fashion enterprises, both in conjunction with Schiaparelli and independently, for they were the natural expression of a Surrealist dandy.

MARCEL VERTES
Rendering of Backward Suit, by Elsa
Schiaparelli, 1937–38
Published *Harper's Bazaar*, New York,
March 15, 1938

When *Harper's Bazaar* published this drawing
of Schiaparelli's innovative suit, it commented:
"A charming little street number, remarkable
only because it is worn front to back." However,
Schiaparelli's suit, with its paradox of
entrances and exits, is certainly more than
slightly remarkable.

JEAN-CHARLES DE CASTELBAJAC
(French, born Morocco 1950)
Backward Suit, 1980

Taking Schiaparelli as his point of departure (or
arrival), Castlebajac created a new suit of
reverse illusionism.

KARL LAGERFELD
Backward Suit, 1986
Photograph Albert Watson

LEFT
HORST P. HORST
Fashion Photograph, 1947

The artistic vocabulary of revised classical forms, deep landscape, and figures both suspended and propped up in Dali's painting *Dematerialization of the Nose of Nero* (1947) were addressed by Horst in his fashion photograph.

BELOW LEFT
HORST P. HORST
Dresses by Adele Simpson, 1943
Published *Vogue*, New York, March 1, 1943

Fashion models pose before the Dali mural in the New York apartment of Helena Rubinstein. Although the transport of figures to the vast world of Dali landscape is only an illusion, the clothing gains clarity and importance from its relation to the world of painting.

OPPOSITE
HORST P. HORST
Costumes by Dali for *Bacchanale*, Ballets Russes de Monte Carlo, 1939
Photograph

In costumes designed by Dali and executed in the studios of Chanel, real figures are incarnated as the limp forms of Dali's imagination.

PAUL DYSON (British, born 1951)
Window Display, Harvey Nichols, London,
1985
Photograph Anthony Lawrence

With a limp, crutch-supported head, a
disintegrated figure, and a mannequin
transformed into a flower, the London display
window uses Dali as the source of inspiration.

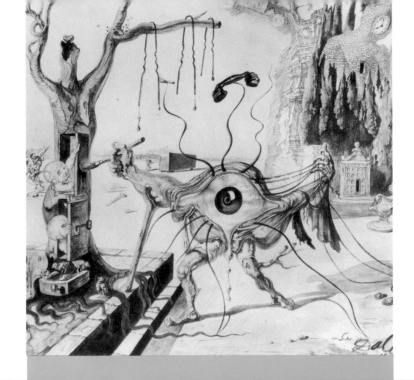

RIGHT
SALVADOR DALI
The Painter's Eye, 1941
Watercolor and ink on paper
Collection Joseph and Jory Shapiro, Chicago

In a summary of favorite themes, from bobby
pins to drawers and cabinets, Dali presented
himself as the all-seeing, all-visual artist.

ABOVE
TOM LEE (American, 1909–1971)
Window Display, Bonwit Teller, New York,
1938

Inspired by the *Trompe l'Oeil* exhibition at the
Julien Levy Gallery, New York, Lee's window is
one of many inflected by Surrealism in America
in the 1930s and 1940s.

LEFT
DAVID BAILEY (British, born 1938)
Fashion Photograph, 1980
Published *Vogue Italia*, Milan, September 1,
1980

After some four decades, Dali's magical
landscapes still provide a place to present high
fashion.

BELOW AND OPPOSITE
SALVADOR DALI
"Dream vs. Reality," 1944
Published *Vogue*, New York, February 15, 1944

Both Dali's imaginary dress and the real one are
transformed by the Surrealist sensibility and
ambience. Although *Vogue* titles the article
"Dream vs. Reality," the two seem more
amicable than adversarial, reality being like a
dream and the dream being akin to the real.

Dream vs. Reality

SALVADOR DALI draws a dream, above.

A dress sketched in over a page torn from a mediaeval

tome on birds and bats and curious beasts.

At the right, Dali draws an existing,

flesh-and-blood, size 10 to 18 fashion.

Rose Barrack's navy rayon crêpe

dress; $50. Pink satin shawl; $23.

Henri Bendel; Garfinckel's; L. S. Ayres

LEFT
SHERRY VIGDOR (American, born Germany 1961)
Clock hat, 1985
Photograph Roxanne Lowit

Firm, but otherwise firmly in the tradition of Dali, the clock has a timeless durability as a fashion theme.

RIGHT
SALVADOR DALI
Limp-Watch Pin, 1949
Minami Art Museum, Tokyo

Initiated as motif in painting, but arising from an accessory of dress, the limp watch is returned, by a perverse twist, to the realm of jewelry.

Only in the brain of Salvador Dali
exists the dress above with its curvaceous bosom,
coat-hanger hip-bones, and entomological accessories.
But the dress that he has sketched on the heroic scale
at the left is an original from Henri Bendel.
It is a white silk crêpe dinner and dance dress,
with a hand-embroidered belt of sequins and amber beads,
which puts forth a transparent peplum of loops.

SURREALISM AND THE WORLD OF FASHION

OSCAR DOMINGUEZ (French, born
Spain, 1906–1957)
Armchair, 1937
Wheelbarrow upholstered with red satin
Photograph Man Ray, courtesy Man Ray
Archives, Paris
Published *Minotaure* Paris, vol. 3, no. 10,
Winter 1937

Surrealist artist Dominguez paradoxically
created a wheelbarrow with the attributes of a
sedan chair, in which Man Ray photographed a
model wearing a Madeleine Vionnet evening
gown, further exaggerating the contrast of
elegance and utility. The upholstered comfort of
the wheelbarrow and the charm of the well-
appointed model establish an uneasy and
awkward disjuncture between this presentation
and the customary purposes of the
wheelbarrow.

Surrealism moved decisively into the world of fashion. Appropriating the imagery of fashion and offering it as metaphor,
Surrealism also shared an interest in the nature of clothing and
in the specific characteristics of fashion. Feeling the disap-
proval of the first-generation Surrealists, yet emboldened by
their adventure in reconciling everyday realities with the large
issues of a revolutionary art, major Surrealist figures entered
the realms of fashion, fashion advertising, and window display
in the 1930s and 1940s. The fashion magazine, both in its design and in its advertising, became the chief point of dissemi-
nation for Surrealist style. French, English, and American
fashion periodicals reflected the art movement through the specific invocation of Surrealism or by the adoption of a Surrealist
style in photography, graphics, and design.

To be sure, some Surrealists disavowed the worldliness of a
Surrealism dressed in the mode of fashion, but many partici-
pated in its adventures. Others sought to separate their "commercial" work from untainted efforts, but even these
distinctions could only be vaguely sustained by the late 1930s,
when the popularity of Surrealist expression in the fashion
journals reached its peak. No single editor or art director can
be considered responsible for the attraction of the journals to
Surrealism, so pervasive was its style among the major fashion
publications, most especially *Vogue* and *Harper's Bazaar*.
Jean-Michel Frank, Jean Cocteau, Leonor Fini, Cecil Beaton,
George Hoyningen-Huene, A. M. Cassandre, and Man Ray
were recruited as unlikely missionaries for the stylistic revolution in the unlikeliest of places. That their cause prevailed and
has continued to sustain itself so completely requires a careful
consideration of the nature of Surrealist style as applied to the
fashion arts.

The first austere, programmatic, and exclusionary expressions
of Surrealist art were, like those of the first Futurists and other
artistic reformers, destined to be of short life. What followed
was a style that was more florid and flexible than that of the
founders, but not in the manner of a second generation.
Rather, it was one of accommodation and transformation, allowing for the expression of such real-world values as the primary form rejected. In its rigor, first-generation Surrealist
thinking all but foreclosed the possibility of strict Surrealism
passing to subsequent generations. Nevertheless, the immediate détente of the followers allowed Surrealism to flaunt its stylistic virtuosity in film, fashion, and the commercial media with
a bravado akin to the self-confidence of the first-generation,
manifesto-making Surrealists. Thus, despite its theoretical

premise and severe first definition, Surrealism assured its succession into new forms and new ideas.

But the fundamental ideas of the first generation could be respected, as, for example, in Surrealist film and photography, forms little analyzed or envisioned in their initial phase but crucial to the development of the Surrealist mythos. One such idea was the interpretation of the body. Denied its integrity by dream interpretation and other psychological insights cognitively known to the early Surrealists and frequently present in their work, the interpretation of the body became an abiding Surrealist premise, even beyond its first associations with the literature of psychology. The partial figure, the dislocation of body parts, and the placement of the figure and/or its parts in unanticipated settings were adopted for promotional imagery and for the new imagery of fashion in the 1930s. The conventional wisdom that fashion and its products depend upon novelty for their promotion is insufficient to explain the role assigned to Surrealism, for other art movements of the period might have been selected for the expression of advertising and fashion. The concept of the partial figure could even be attributed to Cubism or Futurism if such were the isolated and single motive of the new advertising of the 1930s.

Rather, it was precisely Surrealism's ability to juxtapose the real and the unreal that made it a primary form for advertising and media expression. Merchandise, in its crassest form, could be seen; the dream of the consumer product, whether fashion or otherwise, could also be envisioned. The simultaneity of an optical truth and its dreamed doppelgänger could render the product enticing. Photography had long sought to portray the fashion object as desirable within the constraints of the cam-

era's eye. Just as photography was a late, but essential, form of Surrealism, so fashion photography found an ideal style in Surrealism. Not only did Surrealist dress provide a perfect play of illusions, but even the most ordinary garment could be rendered magical in the transformations of a Surrealist photograph. In some measure, the same possibilities obtain for Surrealist illustration.

Surrealism's unattainable dreams, the aestheticization of the product, and the transmogrification of the object were evident in fashion editorial and advertising imagery of the 1930s and 1940s. Its commercial matrix lay in the product and advertising, but it also had an influence in all editorial areas including the covers of such fashion periodicals as *Harper's Bazaar* (United States and England), *Vogue*, and *Flair*, the last of these being Surrealism's great continuing stronghold among fashion publications into the 1950s. *Flair*'s die-cut covers, allowing a reading from exterior into interior, begged for Surrealist invention, and the magazine's close association with Dali fostered dreams of sublime Surrealist women, flower transformation, and splendid plumage.

But Surrealist invention had a more fundamental effect than the simple adornment of pages with butterflies, fluid figures, and the phantasms that could be made to surround apparel. The Surrealist designer would create an entire environment of the magazine page, often with a motif unifying text and image. Surrealism was unafraid of the word and accustomed, even in its earliest forms, to integrating it with the image; the magazine page posed no threat but rather provided an opportunity, especially as the programmatic nature of early Surrealism could be made to serve the adornments of another generation. Fur-

GEORGE HOYNINGEN-HUENE
(American, born Russia, 1900–1968)
Gown by Elsa Schiaparelli, 1939
Photograph
Published *Harper's Bazaar*, New York,
September 1, 1939

Converging here are three artists, the
photographer Hoyningen-Huene, the painter
Leonor Fini (who designed the armoire in the
background), and the clothing designer
Schiaparelli, in a twentieth-century
Gesamtkunstwerk involving a cross section of
the arts. In the 1930s, fashion magazines
particularly encouraged such collaborations
around themes of Surrealist dress and style. The
unaccustomed silhouette of the Schiaparelli
gown, offering a bustle in the front, seems
appropriate in a setting filled with artistic
presences.

GEORGE HOYNINGEN-HUENE
Gown by Alix, 1939
Photograph
Published *Harper's Bazaar*, New York,
September 1, 1939

In the same campaign of photographs, Eugene
Berman provides the set for the gown by Alix
Grès (born 1899).

EDOUARD BENITO (French, born Spain,
1892–?)
Sketch for Gowns by Coco Chanel and Elsa
Schiaparelli, 1938
Published *Vogue*, New York, July 15, 1938

Arcane but elegant, Benito's setting for dresses
by Chanel and Schiaparelli is a translation of
Surrealist landscapes by Dali.

CECIL BEATON (British, 1904–1980)
Lady in Hat Box, 1932
Courtesy Sotheby's, London

thermore, the artistic license of Surrealism sanctioned the freedom that has come to be a characteristic of fashion
publications but had not prevailed before. To see the entire
page as an aesthetic field, disregarding borders associated with
type, was not only to create a fantasy, but also to permit the
synthesis of illustration, photography, and type within the aesthetic assembly of the page. Not only were the Surrealists employed by the fashion magazines, but advertising and editorial
materials employed the devices of Surrealism with a startling
ardor. Simulations of Surrealist space, motifs, and even paintings became—and still are today—frequent devices of fashion
presentation. The Surrealist graphic moved adroitly from manifesto to merchandise.

What was realized in magazines regarding both merchandise
and art was recognized in window display as well. The Surrealist metaphor of the window as eye would seem to be vitiated
when it becomes the place of merchandise instead, but its inventive possibilities were explored by numerous artists and designers. Although Dali's notorious exploits at New York's
Bonwit Teller in 1939—when his Night and Day tableaux

ABOVE AND OPPOSITE
LEONOR FINI (Italian, born Argentina, 1908)
Sketches for Evening Gowns by Elsa
220 Schiaparelli, 1940

Published *Harper's Bazaar*, New York, March 15, 1940

Surrealist painter Fini, who had earlier designed the Shocking flacon for Schiaparelli, illustrates two of the designer's evening gowns for an article in *Harper's Bazaar*. Fini was one of the artists most closely associated with Schiaparelli.

ABOVE LEFT
SALVADOR DALI (Spanish, born 1904)
A Dream about an Evening Dress

BELOW LEFT
GIORGIO DE CHIRICO (Italian, born
Greece, 1888–1978)
La Femme Antique

ABOVE RIGHT
PAVEL TCHELITCHEW (American, born
Russia, 1898–1957)
A Room in a Seashell

Published *Vogue*, New York, March 15, 1937

Three "photo-paintings" commissioned by
Vogue to involve artists in the presentation of
fashion.

COUNTERCLOCKWISE FROM TOP
LEONOR FINI (Italian, born Argentina, 1908)
ALEXEI BRODOVITCH (American, born Russia, 1898–1971)
MIGUEL COVARRUBIAS (Mexican, born 1904)
A. M. CASSANDRE (French, born the Ukraine, 1901–1968)
GIORGIO DE CHIRICO

Hat Boxes
Published *Harper's Bazaar*, New York, March 1937

In 1937 *Harper's Bazaar*, where Brodovitch was then art director, invited artists and designers to create hat boxes for a spring issue. Artists as various as de Chirico, Yasuo Kuniyoshi, and Alexander Calder were invited to take part. Their willingness to be involved suggests a particular indulgence of the commercial aspect of design seldom found earlier in the century—or later. The five artists here all had Surrealist connections, de Chirico as precursor, Cassandre and Covarrubias as illustrators, Fini as illustrator and designer, and Brodovitch as art director.

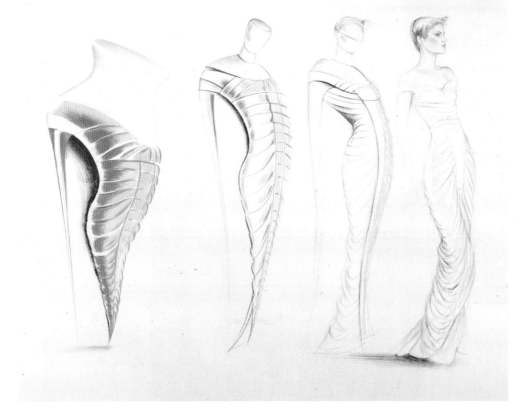

were expurgated by the powers-that-be of the store—tested the idealism of the display notion, they also exerted a lasting influence on the great display artists Tom Lee, Candy Pratts Price, and Gene Moore, revealing the importance of Surrealism for display design. To realize a world within the window, to peer in and through reflectively and reflexively, makes of the window display a magical mirror of Surrealist intent. Like the magazine page, its promotion of a product or an idea external to the art does not exclude Surrealism or make it implausible; rather Surrealism offers the special magic by which the jejune is transformed into the extraordinary. Moreover, window display specifically needed the Surrealist option of transforming scale. The Surrealist symbol existed without reference to scale; thus it enabled the great designers to render the large small and the small large without interrupting the credibility of the scene, whether artificial or real. As the window had served as a visible passage from real to imaginary, so the display window provided a like aperture and like option. To break the window itself, as in a state of pique Dali broke the Bonwit Teller windows in 1939, is merely to make manifest Surrealism at its most transparent.

That Surrealism attained currency in the graphic design of fashion magazines in the late 1930s must also be viewed in the context of cultural history. Impending war and then its presence promoted specific fantasies about fashion. At the time Surrealism offered a mask that was a kind of protective helmet against turbulence. Other styles might offer surcease from war, but no other art could provide the imaginative world of fantasy that the late 1930s and 1940s required. As Schiaparelli had been drawn to Surrealist motifs in 1937 and 1938, coinciding with those years when Europe became aware of the inevitability of war, so too the rapid popularization of Surrealism as a graphic style may have been prompted by the need to provide some fantasied alternative to the bleak prospect of war. As Europe fell, Schiaparelli went to the circus; as Fascism flourished, Surrealism flowered.

Amid such grim realities, one of the options Surealism offered in the fashion magazines was color. The Surrealist palette was Dali's gaiest legacy, along with a strong sense of line. Pastel washes of color were used in Surrealist illustrations to give a shimmer of translucent color; the thin paint of Dali's canvases and of much Surrealist facture translated easily to the magazine page. Of course, such color was neither a universal nor an early trait of the Surrealists but characterized the work of only a few of the more decorative painters in the period. To some degree, Surrealism was an evasion for the fashion magazines of the 1930s and 1940s, allowing them to provide pretty images in the guise and mufti of art. In a brief Hollywood fling at about the same time, Surrealism was likewise a flamboyant and colorful art superimposed on the realities of cinema.

But in all its forms, even with its worldly evasion, Surrealism afforded the same friction between a sinister and a benign vision as it had at its first conception. When Fascism and the Third Reich supplanted the Surrealist dreams with even more potent and powerful horrors, Surrealism did not describe the nightmare directly but kept faith with its instinct to fibrillate the tissues of illusion and reality.

RENE MAGRITTE (Belgian, 1898–1967)
The Castle in the Pyrenees, 1959
Oil on canvas, 78 ¾ × 55 in.
Collection Harry Torczyner, New York

Magritte's vision of a castle in the Pyrenees
plays on the expressions "castles in the air" and
"castles in Spain," merging the two in one
visionary, antigravitational experience of a
giant stone with castle floating above the sea, a
seemingly celestial elevation.

EDWARD MARTINEZ (American, born
1954)
Window Display, Jessica McClintock, San
Francisco, 1985

The adaptability of the Magritte image is
demonstrated in another window display that
achieves the same astonishing feats of levitation
as the original.

ABOVE
ISSEY MIYAKE (Japanese, born 1938)
Dress with Fictive Granite Accessories,
1986–87
Photograph Tahara Keiichi

The stone bag held by the model creates the
physical illusion of weight and gravity, as does
the apparently heavy stone bracelet she wears.
Miyake's knowing wit may well allude to the
weight of garments as well as to Magritte's art
of the heavy stone.

RENE MAGRITTE
Golconda, 1953
Oil on canvas, 31⅞ × 39⅜ in.
Private collection

Magritte's rain of figures has a familiar air yet creates a feeling of acute discomfort. His images have been successfully appropriated by many artists in the fashion arts, most especially Guy Bourdin, whose mysterious images of shoes are often set in a Surrealist perspective.

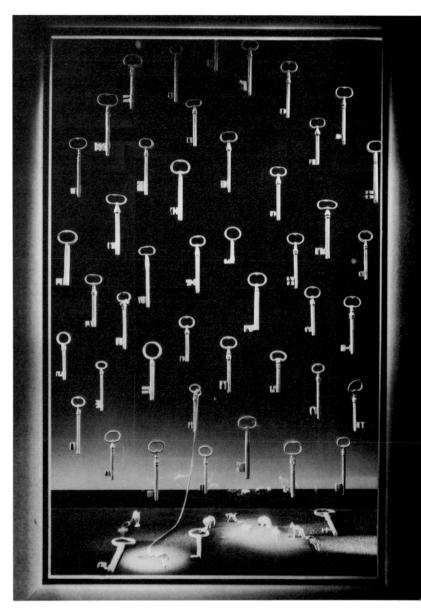

A. M. CASSANDRE
Cover for *Harper's Bazaar*, New York,
March 1937

Posing as the "key to the Paris openings," this
issue of *Harper's Bazaar* purports to be a
special guide for the cognoscenti. It is true that
a magazine can claim to provide special insights
and access to a different world for which the key
is an apt symbol; but Cassandre also opens up
the dreaming world of the Surrealists, suggested
here in the spatial aperture to the blue skies
beyond.

GENE MOORE (American, born 1910)
Window Display, Tiffany & Co., New York,
1962

Moore reveals a special affinity for the devices
and models of Surrealism in using keys to create
a Magrittean harmony.

SAUL LEITER (American)
Dress by James Galanos, 1960
Photograph
Published *Harper's Bazaar*, New York,
November 1960

All seeing but always more passive than overtly
sentient, the Magrittean male spectator
becomes the lambent witness to new fashion,
the observer who is there whether he is
acknowledged or not.

TOP RIGHT
BARRY LATEGAN (American, born South
Africa, 1935)
Fashion Editorial for Cafra Men's Clothing,
1980
Published *Uomo Harper's Bazaar*, Milan,
December 1980

In this instance the male spectator—with vision
obscured by nature—becomes the wearer.

CENTER RIGHT
SHOJI UEDA (Japanese, born 1913)
Formal Wear by Takeo Kikuchi for Men's Bigi,
1983–84
Photograph

Rake, clown, and witness, the singular man in a
bowler hat and a Surrealist landscape is a study
in contrasts between his formality and his
gravity-defying hat trick.

BOTTOM RIGHT
RENE MAGRITTE
Pandora's Box, 26 × 30 in.
Yale University Art Gallery, New Haven,
Connecticut. Gift of Dr. and Mrs. John A. Cook

Magritte's stranger-spectator passes cryptically
through the world of appearances. Fashion
enters his purview, perhaps, through the
flower, which is the transmogrification of
woman and symbol of beauty. His own laconic
presence becomes a type for the male spectator
in contemporary fashion.

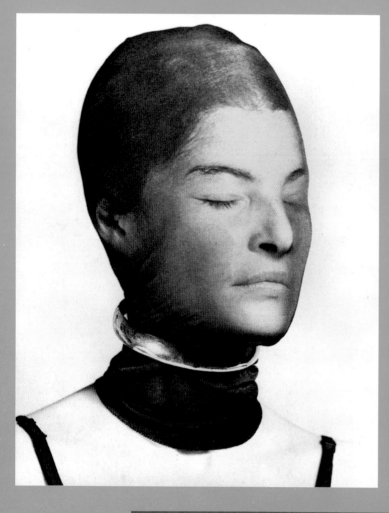

TOP RIGHT
RENE MAGRITTE
The Lovers, 1928
Oil on canvas, 21 ⅜ × 28 ⅞ in.
Collection Richard S. Zeisler, New York

TOP LEFT
MAN RAY (American, 1890–1976)
Portrait of Juliet, c. 1945
Photograph
Man Ray Archives, Paris

BOTTOM
KURT SELIGMANN (American, born
Switzerland, 1900–1962)
Cave of Echoes, 1941
Ink and collage, 20 × 16 in.
Museum of Contemporary Art, Chicago
Gift of Katharine Kuh

The metamorphosis from the wrapped to the
beautiful occurs in fashion and art.

RIGHT
JEAN-FRANÇOIS LEPAGE (French, born 1960)
Fashion Editorial, 1985
Published *Per Lui*, Milan, December 1985

Overtly and cannily Surrealist, a menswear photograph seeks differentiation for men's formal wear through a masquerade both sinister and silly.

BELOW
LOUISE DAHL-WOLFE (American, born 1895)
Fashion Photograph of Claire McCardell Bathing Suit
Published *Harper's Bazaar*, New York, May 1948

GEORGE HOYNINGEN-HUENE

Gown by Elsa Schiaparelli, 1935
Photograph
Published *Harper's Bazaar*, New York,
October 1935

Looking away, as if in longing for some ineffable
beauty, the elegantly gowned model stands in a
Surrealist landscape, the legacy of an artistic
vision to which the world of fashion would
cling in the 1930s.

ACKNOWLEDG-MENTS

It is a paradox that Surrealism, now in its seventh decade, should have so many adherents. Listed below are the designers, photographers, illustrators, publishers, museum curators, dealers, and collectors who have contributed so generously to this book:

Eric Beamon; Anne-Marie Beretta, Anne Vernin; Tom Binns; Manolo Blahnik, Jamie Preito; Judy Blame; Mary Bright; Roberto Capucci; Pierre Cardin; Jean-Charles de Castelbajac, Marc Boisseuil; Bill Cunningham; Eduardo Costa; Jean-Rémy Daumas, Sasha Walckhoff, Laurent Fuchel; Doline Dritsas; Emmé, Claire Krischok; English Eccentrics, Helen Littman, Sandra Kay; John Galliano, Amanda Grieve; Jean-Paul Gaultier, Frédérique Lorca; Tan Giudicelli, Frank Weill, Beatrice Keller; Hubert de Givenchy, Dominique Sirop; Georgina Godley, Sandra Stagg; Olivier Guillemin; Pam Hogg; Marc Jacobs, Robert Duffy; Stephen Jones; Charles Jourdan, Jean-Marie Imoucha, Rosemary Heon; Takeo Kikuchi; Marina Killery; Adam Kurtzman, James Bacchi; Christian Lacroix, Jean-Jacques Picart; Dominique Lacoustille; Karl Lagerfeld, Ralph Toledano, Sarah Matthew, Caroline Cebal; Lederer, Philippe A. Bigar; François Lesage; Adelle Lutz, Andrea Starr; Maidenform, Marcia Cacaci; Pink Soda, Mandy Martin; Issey Miyake, Jun Kanai; Claude Montana, Beatrice Paul; Robert Lee Morris, Sybil Nakamura; Thierry Mugler, Jean-Luc Suchet, Alix Malka; Jean Patou, Jean de Mouy, Patrick Pradelie; Eric Rhein; Marcel Rochas, Hélène Rochas, Monique Berger; Cinzia Ruggieri, Anne Vickerson; Yves Saint Laurent, Pierre Bergé, Stephen de Pietri; David Shilling; Shiseido, Mari Chihaya; Larry Shox; Vivienne Westwood; Kirsten Woodward; Sherry Vigdor; Kansai Yamamoto.

Josef Astor; David Bailey, Sarah Lane; Martin Brading; Alfa Castaldi; Roman Cieslewitz; Jean-Yves Cornec; Maria Vittoria Corradi; Louise Dahl-Wolfe; Willo Font; Scott Heiser; Hideoki; Taishi Hirokawa; Noelle Hoeppe; Horst P. Horst, Rick Tardiff; Daniel Jouanneau; Art Kane, Lisa Garcia; William Klein; Kim Knot, Julian Saddon; Tom Kublin; Barry Lategan; Anthony Lawrence; Saul Leiter; Jean-François Lepage, Susan Dalton; Annie Leibovitz, Rossett Herbert; Roxanne Lowit, Orlando King; Serge Lutens, Patrice Lerat; Niall McInerny; Iain McKell, Sue Odell; Robert Mapplethorpe; Harry Meerson; Christopher Moore; Davide Mosconi; Claus Ohm; Cindy Palmano; Herb Ritts; Michael Roberts; Sheila Rock; Paolo Roversi; David Seymour–Magnum, Elizabeth Gallen; Melvin Sokolsky, Jordan Calfus; Irving Solero; Lance Steadler, Michele Filomino; Bert Stern, Pamela Reed; Keiichi Tahara; Alastair Thain; Christophe-Tony Thorimbert; Oliviero Toscani, Jackie Fixot; Michael Tropea; Shoji Ueda; Tony Viramontes; Paul Warchol; Albert Watson, Peter Schub; Bruce Weber, Nan Bush.

Gabriella Giandelli, Lorenzo Matotti; Antonio Lopez, Juan Ramos, Matthew Olzak; Mel Odom; George Stavrinos.

Mrs. E. A. Bergman, Robert Bergman; Galerie Beyeler; Birch and Conran Fine Art, James Birch; Edwynn Houk Gallery, Edwynn Houk, Sandra Newton; Mrs. Robert B. Mayer, Laurie A. Stein; Robert Miller Gallery, Howard Read; Herbert and Dolores Neumann; Mr. and Mrs. Marshall Padorr; Antony Penrose; Drs. William and Martha Heineman Pieper, Alan Cohen; Kathleen Lamb for the Mr. and Mrs. David C. Ruttenberg Collection and the Richard L. Sandor Collection; Katherine S. Shamberg; Joseph and Jory Shapiro; Sotheby's, London, Lydia Cullen; Staley-Wise Gallery, Ethelene Staley, Taki Wise; Harry Torczyner; Zabriskie Gallery, Virginia Zabriskie, Pamela Salisbury, Ann Lapides; Richard S. Zeisler.

Barney's, Simon Doonan; Henri Bendel, Danuta Ryder; Bonwit Teller; Bloomingdale's, Candy Pratts Price, Jackie Dunham; Calish Associates, Patricia Jefferies; Delman, Howard Nevelow; Sara Tomerlin Lee; Jessica McClintock, Edward Martinez; R. H. Macy, Linda Fargo; Harvey Nichols, Paul Dyson; Portantina Boutique, Barbara Bergreen, Machado and Silvetti; Saks Fifth Avenue, Michael Passantino, Bill Lorenzen; Tiffany & Co., Gene Moore.

The Art Institute of Chicago, T. Faulkner-Lavelle, Kristy Stewart, Julia Bernard; The Brooklyn Museum, Elizabeth Ann Coleman, Polly Willman, Marguerite Lavin; The Metropolitan Museum of Art, New York, Jean Druesedow, Beth Alberty, Kim Fink, Katell le Bourhis; Minami Art Museum, Tokyo, Masao Nangaku, Mr. Ohtake; Musée de la Mode et du Costume de la Ville de Paris, Guillaume Garnier; Musée des Arts Décoratifs, Paris, Daniel Marchesseau; Musée des Arts de la Mode, Paris, Pierre Provoyeur, Florence Müller, Nicole Monsajon; Museum of Contemporary Art, Chicago, I. Michael Danoff, Terry Neff, Alice Piron; The Museum of Modern Art, New York, Mary Corliss, Thomas Grischkowsky; Philadelphia Museum of Art, Dilys E. Blum, Monica Brown; The Tate Gallery, London; Graham Lington; Salvador Dali Museum, Saint Petersburg, Florida, Joan Kropf; Victoria and Albert Museum, London, Sir Roy Strong, Garth Hall, Valerie Mendes, Mark Haworth-Booth; Wadsworth Atheneum, Hartford, Connecticut, Marianne Carlano, Gregory Hedberg, David Parrish; Yale University Art Gallery, New Haven, Connecticut.

Condé Nast, Diana Edkins, Cindy Cathcart, Elaine M. Shaw; Edizioni Conde-Nast Italia, Alda Premoli, Luca Stoppini, Mariuccia Casadio, Micheline Roth; *The Face*, Robin Derrick, James Truman; *Harper's Bazaar*, Martin Schrader, Anthony Mazzola, Susan P. Goodall; *Harper's-Queen*, Hamish Bowles; *i-D*, Stephanie Crean, Peter Brown; *Life*, Deborah Cohen; Mondadori Press, Sandy Auriti; *Paper*, Kim Hastreiter; *Playboy*, Tom Stabler, Holly Binderup, Mary Fennel, Barbara Hoffman; *Uomo Harper's Bazaar*, Mary Cavaglia; *Vanity Fair*, Valerie Sonnenthal, Heather Crocker; *Visual Merchandising*, Laurel Harper; *The World of Interiors*, Nicolette le Pelley.

Suzanne Bartsch; Tina Chow; Charles Cowles; Nancy Hall-Duncan; Janus Films, Karen Rosen; Marie-Andrée Jouve; Kitchen, Kazuko Koike, Setsuko Takeuchi; Judith Mallin; Anne de Margerie; Caroline Reynolds Milbank, Mark Walsh; Studio Berçot, Marie Rucki, François Charles-Domine, Juan Stottani, George Rucki; Juliet Man Ray, Jerome Gold; Lucien Treillard; Pierre Gassman; Dianne Benson.

At the Fashion Institute of Technology, Richard McComb, Dorothy Rudzki, and Tomoko Wheaton made extraordinary contributions to the book through their steadfast and fast research. Barbara Castle and Stacy Broser maintained manuscripts, emendations, and composure with unfailing equanimity. The staff of the Shirley Goodman Resource Center at the Fashion Institute of Technology assisted in countless ways.

At Rizzoli International Publications, Lauren Shakely and William Dworkin were unequivocal in showing faith and giving aid; Sarah Burns contributed patient and painstaking research; Charles Davey saved the design day with acute sensibility for Surrealism and his sure and beautiful ideas for the book; and Jane Fluegel was the omniscient Surrealist eye providing editorial scrutiny and vision in complete professionalism and happy friendship.

Harold Koda and Laura Sinderbrand are my colleagues, co-curators, and true co-authors. They are my best friends. They have my appreciation, admiration, and affection.

R. M.

INDEX

Page numbers in italics indicate illustrations.